the relationship

book one

by Laura Clark

Cradle Press
P.O. Box 8401
St. Louis, MO 63132

Copyright © 2017 Laura Clark
All Rights Reserved

No part of this book may be reproduced, stored in a retrieval system, or transmitted by any means without the written permission of the author and the publisher.

ISBN: 978-0-9979537-1-8
Library of Congress Control Number: 2018934258

Cover Design: Just Ink and Laura Clark

This book is printed on acid free paper.

* *Special thanks to Jane Guenther for her insight.*

In memory of my sister, Pam

* Disclaimer *

This book is as much about relationship as a personal and collective human experience, as it is about relationship with God. While I am a practicing Catholic, my experience in my relationship with God lends me no authority to speak on behalf of the Catholic Church regarding Church teachings. Though I sometimes mention or refer to these teachings, I by no means aim to instruct the reader herein. The best source for instruction in Catholic Church teachings can be found in one of the most beautiful books I have ever read:
The Catechism of the Catholic Church.

Dear Reader †

Interacting in relationships is a universal aspect of human of life. While we have all kinds of relationships with people, this series of books is intended for the reader to question and reflect on: "What exactly is my relationship with God?" For the believer, it is a relationship based on faith, presence; for the nonbeliever, it is a relationship based on disbelief, absence. Acceptance and rejection, belief and lack of belief are equally viable perspectives from which to contemplate the relationship. I welcome readers of all faiths, religious and spiritual practices, agnostics, secularists, and atheists alike. We are naturally inclined to compare and contrast ourselves to others in our human relationships. We can do the same when respectfully considering the relationship with God.

The reflections I offer herein focus primarily on the *dynamics* of the relationship with God – dynamics that are unlike anything we know or experience in human relationships. I offer these reflections because, to my great surprise, I discovered the relationship with God *is actually a real and personal relationship*, not some cliché or figurative construct. But it is not a real and personal relationship because I say so or because any religion says so. I am not writing these books because I found God, but because He found me. Hunted me down is a more accurate statement. Were I to have found Him, these books could never reach beyond the superficial version of the relationship. You know the one – girl is lost, desperate, so she finds God to feel found. I did not arrive in the relationship entirely by my own doing, thinking, reading, believing, or experiencing. If I had, that would mean it is just another human generated relationship, fabricated and defined by my human self. It is precisely because God pursued me that I was opened by His grace to the relationship. In fact, He found me when I most vehemently rejected Him.

While I have always believed in the Trinitarian God (Father, Son, and Holy Spirit), I have lived a mostly secular life. I was raised Catholic, but was away from the Church for decades. I rarely went to Mass and had no real grasp on Church teachings. Interestingly, God began revealing the relationship to me years *before* I returned to the Catholic Church. He moved in my life with subtlety, without any formal context or religion. It would be unfair of me to pretend that Catholicism has no influence on my approach to the relationship. It would be equally unfair of me to withhold how truly taken aback I was that the relationship eventually led me back to the Church – and how floored I was at the ways in which the relationship blossomed into new, deeper dimensions once I did return. It is a richness I never fathomed.

While I will share bits of my story, the bulk of the content herein focuses on the dynamics of the relationship. Certainly my own experiences will color my perspectives and interpretations, but there are many ways we can explore common ground within these dynamics. Too often, an ingrained defense mechanism prevents us from realizing that it is safe for us to reflect openly on God. Regardless if we are believers or nonbelievers, the beauty of the relationship is that it is optional, thus we can contemplate it from within freedom, not obligation or embarrassment. I have no particular agenda, other than to approach God from within the common ground of relationship itself, as a way of uniting us from within our differences, rather than dividing us. My hope is to be able to shed light on aspects of the relationship that secular readers may not have considered. Catholic readers (practicing or lapsed) will perhaps benefit in both their personal relationships with God and with the Church. For readers of other religions or spiritual practices, my wish is that these books speak to you in ways that both reaffirm and surprise you in your spiritual journeys. And, I believe that it is as worthwhile for atheist readers to broaden their perspective about those of us who believe in God, as it is for those of us who believe in God to broaden our perspectives about those who do not believe. The beauty of the relationship is that it neutralizes all our differences.

The relationship surpasses all human stereotypes, explanations, alliances, and expectations. We normally process the idea of having a relationship with God by way of belief, faith, emotions, the intellect, reason, and logic. However, the substantive nature of the relationship extends far beyond our human capacity to define and explain. Belief, lack of belief, faith, lack of faith, proof, lack of proof – these are all human standards of measurement. If we attempt to form our relationship with God by strictly human constructs (measuring, qualifying, quantifying, defining), we are assembling our own version of truth about the relationship from within the limitations of being human. God's presence in the relationship is not something *we* can determine, because we are not the source of it.

Before we delve into the dynamics of the relationship, in *Part One* we "get our sea legs" so that you can consider your own beliefs (or lack thereof) about God. *Part Two* is designed to flesh out the dynamics, so that you can reflect on how they manifest in the relationship with God. And *Part Three* is about moving forward in the relationship, from within your own faith or practice.

The relationship itself is not God; I am in no way advocating any kind of idolatry. Rather, this exploration hinges on the relationship as a context, a framework within which we dwell – the architecture of creation, so to speak. The best any of us can do is to simply share the gifts bestowed. I am able to write words for you to ponder, but I can no more give you the relationship from a series of books than you can receive it from me by reading them. Let us together discover.

~ Laura Clark

Stylistic note: You will notice I bounce around in my use of pronouns. It is not my intention to make accusations, sweeping generalizations, or to assume you fall into certain categories or behaviors (know that I include myself as part of the "we" to whom I refer). Nor is it my desire to proselytize. I alternate pronouns solely for the purpose of being consistently conversational in tone. Likewise, the grammar police are sure to come knocking since my subject/verb agreement is also rendered conversational.

† Table of Contents †

Part 1 ~ Living Within Living

Chapter One ~ Other and Same 1

Chapter Two ~ G 8

Chapter Three ~ Reciprocity 11

Chapter Four ~ Defective Defect 17

Chapter Five ~ Reckoning 24

Chapter Six ~ Faith 31

Chapter Seven ~ Condition Critical 36

Part 2 ~ Sacred Dynamics

Chapter Eight ~ Initiation 45

Chapter Nine ~ Conversion 52

Chapter Ten ~ Revelation 62

Chapter Eleven ~ Grace 67

Chapter Twelve ~ The Word 79

Chapter Thirteen ~ Salvation History 88

Part 3 ~ Pathways to Yes

Chapter Fourteen ~ Fiat 97

Chapter Fifteen ~ S 105

Chapter Sixteen ~ Passion 113

Chapter Seventeen ~ Assumed and Genuine 117

Chapter Eighteen ~ Fragmentation and Unification ...122

Chapter Nineteen ~ Adhere to Cohere 126

Chapter Twenty ~ The Gift In You 130

Epilogue 135

End Notes 139

Part 1

Living Within Living

Chapter One ~ Other and Same †

*The relationship with God
is at once completely other and same.
It is love in entirety, forever creating and
procreating us, living from within and without.*

Our concept of relationship, in broad strokes, pertains to interacting with, communicating with, connecting with others. Human to human relationships are based on otherness and sameness: each of us is an individual; every one of us is human. But no other human being has the capacity to *be* any one else. Only Creator can be both Creator and creation. Thus, the relationship is its own, unique entity. It is not that we are living in relationship with God; rather, God is creating us within a living relationship.

Rather than super imposing any definition or image of God, let us simply consider how a relationship with a higher power shores up with any human to human relationship. At the most basic level, other humans with whom we relate will eventually die, as will each of us. We are finite and the higher power is infinite. That alone sets apart the relationship from human relationships. Regardless if we name the higher power God, Allah, Enlightenment, "The Universe" – or even if we attach no name – we are all in relationship with something far bigger than we are (as individuals, as well as the totality of humanity). And, whatever title or name or pronoun we choose to use when referring to this higher power, we should not confuse the *name* with the relationship. I use the name God and the masculine pronoun, and I am referring to the Holy Trinity. But none of these identifiers, in and of themselves, describes my *relationship* with God, though one could conclude that I am Christian because of the names I use. In our human relationships we do not define the uniqueness in each person's relationship to another by virtue of the names of the people. Likewise, we cannot understand the uniqueness of anyone else's relationship with God by virtue of particular labels.

The relationship is completely organic to self – we cannot help but seek it, albeit we can do so from within a variety of approaches. By delving into the dynamics of the relationship, we can take a fresh look at our human relationships (to self and others), as well as our beliefs regarding the higher power. Will the ego put in its own two cents all along the way – of course; that is its job. It will likely aim to discredit the content herein as a way of preserving control. But rest assured that none of the ego's interjections need interfere, because no threat exists. The relationship is entirely built on love, and love seeks not to damage and destroy, but to liberate and renew.

The Relationship and Religion

Rather than considering the relationship with God from within any external framework (theology, religion, theory, philosophy, spiritual practice), let us consider *relationship itself* as framework. We sometimes place more emphasis on *practicing* the relationship with God within a framework, rather than *living* in it as a relationship. In other words, while we structure all our relationships around frameworks (family, friends, co-workers, etc.), we normally do not relate to the framework as much as we relate to the actual people. Thus, sitting down at a family dinner is more about interacting with those at the table, not with the table itself. While the table gives these interactions temporary locality, we need not carry the table along with us in order for our family relationships to grow and change. Though billions of people of faith experience and interact with God within the framework of religion, none of us is completely reliant upon the religion itself in order to live in the relationship. If we were, nonbelievers could never be converted because, while frameworks may play a part in conversion, they do not, in and of themselves, convert – God does. God comes before all religions, and so too does our relationship with Him, because it does not originate anywhere else except in unity with Him. *It is from within the relationship that we are called.*

No matter if we are raised in a particular faith or no faith, we inevitably are able to choose for ourselves what to believe and not believe. Yet, if any philosophy or religion we practice is simply an external framework within which we choose to participate, it will eventually lack the key motivating ingredient: *intimacy*. Eventually, it becomes difficult to sustain one's faith inside any skeletal structure that is void of the intimate relationship with God. In Western culture, the currently popular hybrid of secularism and religion contains an inherent neutralization. Because each approach tends to invalidate the other, a kind of equal trade-off becomes the operating dynamic. God becomes a convenience or an inconvenience, depending on what one desires at the time. The end result is a rift that is inevitably reflected in every relationship one has; with oneself, others, the world, and God. I lived from within this hybrid relationship for decades. While most aspects of my life were primarily secular, my soul maintained an incessant spiritual exploration. Thus it was a constant canceling out of all questions asked and answered. A hybrid life is, in essence, a life based on deep internal division.

Relativism tells us that we all relate to ourselves and our lives from our own unique truths and perspectives. This often means we end up telling one another how each other "should" live, and we may get quite upset when others choose to live differently than we do. This intolerance of others, even if only subconscious, permeates our human relationships in destructive ways. The irony, of course, is that both relativism and secularism tell us what our truth should be just as much as any religion does. World politics, natural disasters, and human tragedies remind us that much of human life is beyond our control. So we are left scrambling, searching for meaning, or denying that there is any meaning. Our searching and denying reaches into our daily moments, hours, days, weeks, years, decades, centuries, millenniums – and keeps reaching, backwards to the origins of human existence and forwards into our future and beyond.

Rather than concentrating on any particular belief system, spiritual practice or religion, if we first approach God from within the relationship itself as the framework, we begin this journey by standing together on level ground. That way, those of us who are Christian, Jewish,

Buddhist, Secularist, New-Ager, Muslim and so on are not in competition, caught up in external comparative analysis. The obvious question here is "What about the atheist, the non-believer?" Oddly, it is within the relationship with God that believers and nonbelievers have something pivotal in common, in terms of human identity. Consider that much of our identity is shaped around things like our personal relationships and all our "doing." We give names to our relationships and doing: mother, doctor, janitor, student, pilot, and so on. But if we had no human relationships and if we ceased from all doing, how would we identify ourselves? Would believers make the claim: "I am a child of God"? Would non believers profess: "I am not a child of God"? or "I am a child of nothing"? Our lives pared down, we all end up with the same basic question: "Who am I?"

God does not exist merely because we cannot explain the lack of His existence. And because we lack the ability to adequately prove exactly *how* God exists, does not mean that He does not exist. Because God is a mystery to us, we are a mystery to ourselves, regardless if we "believe" in Him or not. Thus, the relationship is worth exploring if, for no other reason, than to have a deeper understanding of ourselves and our human relationships.

In retrospect, I am aware that, for decades, I maintained and defended a limited, human-based perspective about life. Having a relationship with God seemed to me to be an idea that was based mostly on human perception, belief, hope, the need for reassurance, and blind faith (some would add delusion to the list). It involved living as a human being in a fabricated relationship with an entity that was hierarchical, antithetical. It was comprised of reverence and absolute

the relationship

trust in God, and then following a lot of rules to be part of a particular religion. Over the years, I studied many philosophies, religions, and spiritual practices, none of which had any staying power. At some point with each, I hit a wall then moved on in my quest for answers. Fed up, I found no sanctuary in either belief or disbelief. It was not until I was totally cornered, with no way in or out of myself, that I stopped all efforts at trying to make sense out of it and eased up on my quest for answers. Eventually though, the lack of structural integrity in the self I had become bore the ache of something missing that had always been there. In truth, God had been making inroads in our relationship throughout my entire life, in both my doubts and my hopes. I was simply unaware.

As God continued building our relationship, I slowly became more of a participant than an observer. What now fascinates me most is how counter-intuitive it is that *the* most important relationship in our lives is so often not actually *lived*. The living relationship creates itself perpetually because the focus has shifted from self, onto God and others. It then develops incrementally into a deeper self, *with* God and others. And the wheel goes round. Each part of the relationship is inter-dependent on every other; each aspect constitutes the whole. Equally mysterious, if each of us is in a unique creation-relationship with the Creator, in each relationship the entirety of all relationships is, in essence, accessible (hence one is already hard-wired to love God with all one's heart and love one's neighbor as one's self)."Other" is fleshed out with "same" and becomes its equal. All opposites are reconciled.

Perhaps the greatest challenge for me as the author

and you as the reader is the non-linear realm in which we must reside when contemplating the relationship. Everything is connected to everything else; the relationship is not a step by step progression. It exists outside time, though we experience it as existing in time. Because the relationship is held in constant wholeness, each chapter and each book in this series, though compartmentalized, has an inherent interchangeability – not because I am writing it as such, but because the relationship itself is dynamic, living. Embracing any adventure involves wandering into uncharted regions. Perhaps we would do well to begin by embarking from within the beauty of the following paradox:

The relationship is, at once, distinctly and vastly personal and universal; it is as unique to each of us, as it is inclusive of all of us.

Chapter Two ~ 𝓖 †

It was one of those interruption dreams – the kind that happen when you are in the middle of a long dream and are suddenly transported into another. I was presented with a piece of paper, divided into two columns, and was told to write whatever it was I had to say before I died. The left column had someone's writings on it, so I was given the space on the right. I began to think of frivolous things I could write, in a vain attempt to be clever, funny. But then a serenity came over me and I realized the gravity of the opportunity. Softly, as though by way of an illusory mist, I received certain knowledge that whatever I wrote would be read by millions of people (why they call them dreams, folks). This was to be it, my chance to leave behind something truly worthwhile. I paused and wondered: "What could I write that would be most beneficial to others?" I took the pen and began writing a large, cursive, sweeping, beautiful "G" in the blank space and continued writing the only words of value that I had to communicate:

"God is real!"

I awoke suddenly, but without any residue of impending doom. Rather, I wondered calmly why I had chosen God's "realness" as the most important thing to communicate. And how is God real? Is it because He is truth and truth is reality? And why was God being real such a critical message, especially for our secular world? What are the ramifications of God being real? I drifted back into the morning's tranquility as my mind dallied in the memories of my own recent conversion. What was it that convinced me beyond any shadow of a doubt that God is real?

One word presented itself: *presence*. I came to understand that the primary, fundamental flaw of my secular life was that my relationship with myself could never surpass God's presence in my self. That realness of His presence is what reoriented me in my relationship with Him, with myself, and with others. When writing my sentence in my dream, I was not trying to communicate the importance of *believing* "God is real!" Rather, I knew I was communicating a truth that lies beyond human beliefs. And, though I desired to offer reassurance, encouragement to those who are bound to the limitations of secular lives, I was also keenly aware that, embedded in these words, supposedly my very last words, was the truth of salvation, liberation, the realness of love which *is* God's presence.

One could argue that I am merely imagining God's presence. But imagination and belief can never form truth; truth *is* – period. I cannot create truth by believing anymore than I can deny truth by disbelieving. And, while believing can certainly serve as a springboard, catapulting one towards God's truth, *real* presence can be nothing but real. I can imagine it, believe in it, defy it, sling mud at it – whatever, but I have no ability to define, create, determine, demand, change, shape, control, or possess God's realness, God's presence. I am in a relationship with God and He is in a relationship with me *inside* His presence, His realness, His truth. Even if I do not choose it, the relationship exists because God *always* chooses it. God will not force it on me, but when I opt to choose the relationship, the real presence of God is what brings me into deeper intimacy with Him. It is an intimacy that transcends our narrow definition, in that it does not simply indicate extreme closeness in relationship. It is relationship as real-ationship.

Chapter Three ~ Reciprocity †

When referring to an idea or inanimate object, we often say "My relationship *to*...politics, money, food, alcohol..." and the like. God is not an idea. We have a relationship *with* God, the *"with"* implying unity, connectivity, reciprocity. An idea or a thing cannot, of its own volition, relate back to you; there is no conscious, intentional reciprocity on its part. So, while a dysfunctional relationship *to* food might cause one to be unhealthy, the food itself is not responsible. Likewise, a healthy relationship to food is non-reciprocal. An apple has no say in who takes a bite.

All our human to human relationships have some degree of reciprocity. Being in relationship with someone involves interaction, communication. Being in a relationship with oneself also involves a give and take dynamic. Regardless if this reciprocity in relationship is driven by like or dislike, it is nonetheless an exchange of some sort. Thus we can say that both a devout believer and an atheist have a relationship with God. As previously stated, the former is a relationship based on faith, while the latter is a relationship based on disbelief. Thus, even if atheists consider God to be nothing more than a concept or an illusion, they cannot say with certainty that God is not in relationship with them. They can claim lack of reciprocity only from their side. Their disbelief is, in essence, the *way* they relate *to* God (as a concept). They can have a say as to whether or not they want to take a bite from the apple, but they cannot take away (with their disbelief) God's desire to make them the apple of His eye. If God wants to love, He loves. An atheist might point out that an idea, a concept cannot love. Precisely.

The very fact that love exists in the world reflects the truth that God is real. Equally, the very fact that suffering exists in the world also reflects the truth that God is real. But these books are not meant to be a discourse on the merits of *believing* in God or not. Rather, the focus is on how the realness of God, which is independent of human acceptance, is integral to the relationship itself. Relationship is the axis and apex of love. An atheist cannot love another person unless some degree of relationship exists, even if that other person is a total stranger. Nor can a believer love outside relationship. We all love and suffer from within relationships – with ourselves, with others, with God, and without God. An atheist would likely say that it is entirely possible to love in relationship, with oneself and with another, without being in relationship with God. This would then mean that love is human made. But did humans love the stars into existence? Did we love the sun to shine so that plants grow and we can eat? It is much easier to argue that suffering is man made (since most of it is). But do we create the tornado that destroys? Do we have the ability to extinguish our own death so that our loved ones will not mourn our loss?

As an idea or concept, God is a one dimensional God and, as such, it is easy to dismiss His realness. But the relationship is undeniable on God's end of the equation. Even if we reject the idea of being in relationship with

Him, He will not reject being in relationship with us. For as Creator, he is in relationship with all creation. And we cannot be in relationship with creation without being in relationship with the Lover of all creation. Trees do not try to be anything other than the beauty God created them to be. Nor do they judge themselves when they fall in the forest and decay, returning to the soil from which they grew. Why should any of us be anything less or more than the reflection of God that He created us each to be?

All God's love is always available to us. With Him we are simultaneously emptied and filled. We are emptied in that, whenever we surrender our will to Him, our self-emptying removes the spotlight from us and shines it where it belongs – on God. Our will recedes, once we unify with the swell of His will. We are filled in the sense that, as we empty, He fills us with His all pervasive love. We could never matter more than we matter from within His love – even if our meager self were to live billions of human lifetimes. For without His will at the helm, we are not capable of truly receiving His love. We are simply not big enough to measure it, imagine it, or assimilate it on our own.

Each of us accepts and denies relationships throughout our lifetime, choosing to befriend this or that person and avoiding those with whom we feel no kinship. Our relationships are part of the reason life has become so busy. In *the* relationship, however, in the stillness and permanence of God's presence in our lives, ideas and concepts of Him fade into the background. Regardless of how or when we come into the awareness of being in relationship with God, once we do our lives are elevated, both internally and externally. One's being finds its alignment within the realness of God. And in the realness of God we are liberated by the understanding that, regardless of any efforts to change ourselves, to become more loving and alive, the truth is we cannot change ourselves *by ourselves*. At some point we hit a wall, a kind of paralysis, in which we come to realize that we must allow God's will to replace our own if we are to be truly transformed.

God designed us as conscious beings within the context of relationship. For Him, there is no such thing as an inanimate object or creature, because all particles belong in His being. While seeming boundaries govern our existence in space and time, He permeates all creation. So why is His relationship with humans so special? Why create us with a conscience? To what end? For Him? For us? Here, the theory of evolution can teach us God's logic. Take an amoeba and a man, and God in relationship with both. The kind of reciprocity the amoeba has with its Creator is limited, in that, because the amoeba has no conscience, it cannot *choose* to love God, though it is an *expression* of God's love by virtue of being a creation of God's. Man too is an expression of God's love by virtue of being one of God's creations, but God elevates the love through man's consciousness. Love, no longer merely super-imposed, becomes love chosen. But man cannot choose to love God outside the context of relationship. Sometimes the starkly obvious renders us indifferent to subtle nuance. Choosing to love God as simply an idea and from outside the relationship would mean objectifying God. It would, in essence, be akin to a form of idolatry. This is an intrinsically deficient way of living. One cannot "make" God by virtue of worshiping Him, any more than worship itself can make the person worshiping. Nothing (or no one) we idolize can *sustain us*, due to lack of reciprocity of the love that *creates*.

Choosing to love God in the relationship alters us, and we become co-creators of the relationship. When we explore the many dynamics of being in relationship with God, the many exchanges, communications, interactions and certain connectivity, our lives blossom. *Being* bolsters the dynamic of reciprocity in the relationship.

The theology of the relationship and the relationship itself are one in the same. The familiar context of relationship allows secular and religious readers alike to explore beyond limited intellectual viewpoints or emotionally driven beliefs about God. Naturally we all experience relationships in ways that are unique to each given relationship. So too is each person's relationship with God entirely unique. One of the great ironies of secularism is its obsession with the uniqueness of the self. To shine with the reward of Christ's salvation, for example, seems so counter-intuitive in today's alchemy of self-determination. Secularism is *self*-propelled and *self*-perpetuating. Its influence makes it difficult for both believers and non believers to be in the relationship without placing many conditions on it. Secularism promotes relationships of benefit, convenience, and, most importantly, *self*-fulfillment. Even sacrifices we make in relationships bend towards self-promotion (being considered a "great" mom or dad, wife or husband, lover or friend, co-worker or boss). The lens always captures the selfie.

Because secularism primarily promotes relationship with the self and with life, the self lives in a life-centric relationship (with death as the end, always hovering). Self as the center of one's life and life as the center of one's self is a mutually exclusive relationship. To retain supremacy, the self must perpetuate its life, thus even

the relationship

others become instruments for the self, regardless if the self is giving or taking in relationships with others. But a self dependent solely on life on earth loses the freedom of life everlasting. Life is the creation; life is not the Creator of itself. Life is not God, therefore the self in the relationship with the eternal God far surpasses the self's brief relationship with its destined-to-expire life.

Why would the secular self make life its god of choice? Is the ego reliant upon control to the extent that it must abscond life from the Creator and claim it as its own? The secular self who makes life its god is actually in proximity to the relationship with God, more so than he or she might realize. For when life's challenges arrive and the ego realizes its inherent limited nature and lack of control, God whispers into the ear of the self the nearness of the relationship. God cradles the human soul, reminding the self that a life surrendered to God is a life extended by God.

Chapter Four ~ Defective Defect †

It is easy for me to remember the many struggles I encountered that prevented me from fully embracing the relationship. It was not that I doubted God's existence, but I challenged His means. I lodged into my mind the trick question: "How could a loving God allow all the suffering in the world (mine included)?" I could not comprehend what possible reason He could have for this endless stream of pain and anguish that repeatedly befalls humanity.

I had it out with Him one night, arguing that it was unfair of Him to have us suffer so, given our faulty design was not of our own making. I reasoned that, even if Eve and Adam fell, God was the one Who designed them with the *potential* to fall, to be tempted to raise themselves above Him. I thought of it as being similar to a product that is recalled due to some design defect. It is the company's responsibility to fix the defect; the product cannot fix itself. This theory made it easy for me to blame God for all the sin and suffering in the world. I challenged Him by pointing out that we did not create ourselves, nor did we ask to be created. I indulged and hunkered down, deep inside my anger, and screamed at Him (literally) "You cannot create us with the potential to sin and then turn around and blame us when we do! It is *Your* defective design, thus it is *Your* responsibility!"

Even though I believed that He took responsibility for us by sacrificing His only Son for our sins (meaning every shred of every sin of every person throughout all time), I was so mired in my own suffering that I could not understand why that should suffice. I had endured a series of losses, so I argued that He did not actually *lose* His Son to death, whereas I had (seemingly) forever lost people I loved. At one point, I lashed out irreverently, calling Him a coward for blaming us for any sins (probably hoping He would zap me with a bolt of lightning to end my misery). I even found myself defending all those who had ever hurt me, claiming they were just as victimized as I was by His defective design.

I laugh at myself about this now, but while it was happening I was like a child litigator, screaming at the judge in a wild tantrum. I was *furious* with Him, so deeply hurt that life had to be filled with such suffering and that evil could reign freely. It seemed to me that Jesus hanging on the Cross did not fix a thing with humanity – that we were still totally defective. I declared Him an incompetent God, selfish for having created a problem and making us pay for His mistake. And to make it worse, He had not even given us the *ability* to fix ourselves. I accused Him of having the biggest ego of all, of being a power hungry God who must actually enjoy watching us squirm and suffer and die. I berated Him for all the injustices, accusing Him of being nothing more than a big bully. Knowing I was crossing a line and that there would be no coming back, I unleashed my rage and became vicious. I worked myself into such a frenzy that my outburst inevitably devolved into physical rage. I picked up the iron Crucifix I had received as a child for my First Communion and with my every ounce of strength hurled it across the room.

book one

The *second* it left my hand, I experienced the acute, total undoing of my being. It was the same regret I can only imagine a tortured soul committing suicide must feel the moment of jumping. I immediately understood the ultimate desperation of looking to God to spare the soul from the horrid abyss of separation from Him. The moment stretched out in slow motion as I watched the Crucifix flying through the air. From *within* this moment, the moment I spitefully rejected Him, He revealed an eternal moment of finding me. I burst into tears and sprung up to stop the Crucifix before it hit the wall, but I was too late. I picked it up off the floor. Christ's nailed feet had come dislodged from the Cross. The fact that I had actually damaged it cast a grave shadow of dread onto my own brokenness. More than fear of retribution, the sinking remorse of having committed the worst offense darkened my soul. I was overwhelmed by a sudden surge of guilt for my lack of gratitude. I begged God to forgive me, for every sin, every rebellion, every failing, every doubt, for all of it. I crawled onto my bed and draped my body over Christ's feet, the weight of the shame of my anger and arrogance and pride upon me. I remained there immobile, truly wretched, totally emptied, with nothing left to say or do or be.

After some time, from somewhere buried deep within, I mustered a tiny voice with which to plead with God. From within an authenticity I had never know before, I told Him that there was now *nothing* I could do – that if He wanted me to live, He would have to take over my living. I vowed, with an equal measure of reverence and conviction, that I would never get out of my bed – ever. He would have to do it *for* me, or there I would live and there I would die. Life as the person I had been had become intolerable. I sincerely wanted to change, but knew I was powerless to change myself. I begged Him to rescue me, pleading: "I cannot do it myself. I have nothing left of myself to give." Then I surrendered.

I fell into a deep slumber. When I awoke the next morning, I lay in stillness, emotionally spent but with such clarity of being. Suddenly, I was entirely compelled to get up, go to my computer, and read the Stations of the Cross. I did so and spent a few hours immersed in reading and writing about each of them.

And then I just kept moving.

I share my hysteria and melodrama to point out that anger cannot permanently damage the relationship. A God of love and forgiveness is impervious to anger, violence, and the like. He listens to us with mercy and compassion. Even though I brought my absolute worst to Him, He did not retaliate. As long as I brought it to Him, in the spirit of having a starkly honest dialogue, He had no qualms about me unleashing my rage. What I came to understand is that He longs for us to communicate with Him from within that degree of authenticity and honesty. For Him, the content is not what matters – He can handle whatever we throw (literally) at Him. What matters is that we bring it to *Him*, rather than acting out in the world. This is why the context of the relationship is vital, for within it we live our life *in* Him. Again, this rings obvious. But if we reflect upon it, we will better understand how often, even subconsciously, we separate ourselves from God by objectifying Him, rather than relating with Him. He does not need or want us to idolize Him; His desire is for us to *engage* intimately with Him, in Him, through Him, so that we can know ourselves as being created in His image and likeness.

Though my verbiage is based in Christianity, and may be completely foreign to you, Christians do not have an exclusive contract with God. All mankind was, is, and will be created by God. Each of us has access to the interior, private love of God that nurtures the fullness of each of us as a unique creation, one who is ever ascending in prayer as the heart expands. It is like being a child and having a secret language with your best friend. God's love is the gravitational force that governs the universe. Everything ultimately is converted into goodness through Him. When I hurled that Crucifix, the air, walls, floor, and room became shock absorbers of my bottomed out self. This is what God does with any anger, or sin, or evil, for they are mere echoes of what Christ *already* absorbed for us on the Cross. They *feel* real to us, but the reality is that they have already been rendered hollow of lasting harm. They cannot cause irreparable damage as long as we willingly dwell in the relationship and resolve to do our best to become better human beings. This does not mean that we (or others) will not suffer repercussions from our wrongdoings; but it does mean that, with God, we have always been and will always be loved, even at our worst. And when we hate others or ourselves, God's response will still be love (albeit tough love at times). He is always ready and willing to save us.

Because God gives us the *choice* to be in relationship with Him, we also have the choice to defect from the relationship. We can abandon our homeland in Him and take up residence elsewhere. Indeed, many have defected from the relationship and have emigrated to a life where sin is considered a tired, guilt producing nuisance. The choice to defect, however, temporarily renders the soul

the relationship

defective. For a soul separated from the homeland of its Creator becomes "a stranger in a strange land." What is most challenging to understand is that, like the defective product that cannot fix its own defect, we cannot fix our defect – sin – because Christ already fixed it for us on the Cross. This should come as a relief to us, and sometimes it does, but the ego keeps us in the struggle. The ego likes to assert control, to step into the role of Creator and assert itself as the answer. It also has a difficult time facing its defects because so much of one's self-esteem revolves around the ego's incessant need to be admired and valued. The irony is, of course, that the peak of our worth is in our life with God.

Our attempt to rid ourselves of our defect (sin) extends well beyond the ego. For even when we *choose* God and do our best to live a good life, we can never entirely free ourselves from our sinfulness while on this earth. At times, this has made me feel imprisoned – in myself. The *desire* to live life with God can never be enough, in and of itself. The desire has to be reinforced by our daily declaring and living our "Yes!" to God to the best of our ability, surrendering our will to His. Once surrendered to our dependence on Him, our hearts expand and are taken up in His. He never forces us to surrender our will or our hearts, yet He plants that seed of searching so that we can find His love living inside us.

To complete the word play: our will leans us towards our defect (sin), which is defective in its lack of permanence in God's love and mercy. It is really more the *appearance* of a defect, because within the relationship lives the promise of our salvation. In the same breath, we call ourselves sinners *and* children of God. Yes, we are both, but in God we become whole, unified by

book one

redemption. Our relationship with God is sealed salvific.

Chapter Five ~ Reckoning †

While alive and after we die, we will have been and will continue to be relevant to those who love us. But after they are long gone, we will eventually disappear in humanity's rear view mirror. This is a simple truth, not some morose philosophy or existential angst. Generations will come and go behind us. Only a few people are remembered in the stream of human history. The sum of our individual worth is only bound to eternity through our relationship with God; it is the only place where we have always been and will always be completely relevant.

The risk of believing in and surrendering our lives to God is a terrifying prospect to the self. It is both the beginning and culmination of a dismantling that is, frankly, radical. Our walls begin to shake and we realize that what we thought was our foundation is swiftly crumbling beneath us. We fear being sucked into a vortex, a place where self cannot sustain – itself. It is far easier to occupy ourselves with the many available addictions and distractions in life. And, even if we begin deconstructing the construct of self, that same self will sound the alarm, reminding us that it is *so* much easier to trust oneself than it is to trust God. Our control issues will again storm through the door, guns a blazing. And Our Creator, who made us in His likeness, will be demoted and redefined as being nothing more than an autocratic menace in our lives.

Finding yourself in order to lose yourself and losing yourself in order to find yourself – both seem to be tremendous undertakings. Somehow, we seem to think we will sacrifice ourselves and the fun in life if we turn over our lives to God. It is as though we are worried that near the end of our lives we will realize we have been ripped off – that we could have lived entirely hedonistic lives rather than wasting our time attempting to live holy lives. Whenever we deny the true self, we block access to holiness. We continue to live a lie, alienated from our potential as children of God. We deprive ourselves by knowingly rejecting a co-creative relationship.

If we pay attention to our motivations, we are able to extrapolate the truth of who we are and how we are in the world. And, from within that tenuous reality, we can decide if we are honestly happy or if we are fooling ourselves. We can begin by considering how many relationships, jobs, hobbies, addictions, beliefs, and trends have run their course in our lives. How often do we come to the end of something and grab onto the hope of the next new thing that will occupy our time and satisfy our needs? Or how often do we conclude that we can fix our unhappiness with a new job, relationship, vacation, or purchase? All parts of our lives are impacted from our point of reference and, if our default point of reference is self, we will be living limited, one dimensional lives. Ironically, by obeying the self and all its demands, we minimize existence, making it lusterless and malnourished.

God is every creative composition made and every composition to be made. His is the inhale and the exhale of every living creature. Residing in the relationship, we

the relationship

can perceive the equanimity of every single thread in God's tapestry. All threads are interdependent *and* equally significant. God initiates the relationship and our privilege is to trust and follow. The gate to freedom is ours to open. *No other exit from self offers true freedom* – not drugs, not alcohol, not sex, not money, not an adrenaline rush – no risk we take will ever suffice. These only offer a temporary *sense* of freedom, a feeling of escape. We feel courageous and powerful when we push our edges and explore our darkness in this high-gloss, heavy-grit world.

But when our lives are elevated in the relationship, the fine and fluid edge of truth is at once experiential and cognitive, visceral and tangible. It is an unraveling process of God appearing to disappear to reappear. It is love breathing in being. Denying ourselves life in God is the ultimate example of fear of success. Do we find ourselves so unworthy as to inflate the self to a status that, although grossly inferior, becomes our non-negotiable identity? Self-reliance leaves us careening towards self-destruction. Without life in God, we eventually reside in a dreary state of equanimity, where all the relied upon sources of life ultimately feel dull and fall flat. Why would we ever choose to deny ourselves our unique design, thereby draining our only true life source of God-given, sustaining love?

Since many who live according to secular ideology have deemed life itself to be a kind of god to worship, a sense of entitlement has been attached to human life, especially in Western cultures. The blessing of being, as a God given state, has been transformed into an ownership right, one that can be dismissed at will (think violent crime, abortion, euthanasia, suicide); or it can become the source of ongoing self-indulgence. It is a sharp irony when, in the same breath, one can defend vigorously the rights he or she has to lead a full life, to take advantage of all opportunities, to pave one's own way, and then deny those same rights in another. Ownership breeds exclusivity and binds us to the self. And our ongoing indulgence in the self keeps us hyper-focused on creating and championing a self-made existence. A troubling trend threatening the dignity of the human person is self-deification. If self is the primary point of reference in people's lives, this creates havoc in societies. If self becomes its own god, and there are billions of people in the world, would that not mean that there would be billions of competing gods? Self-deification wears away at the human soul, because bit by bit, one isolates oneself from God. The "lost soul" becomes the soul that must lose itself.

Deconstructing

Through the process of self-reckoning, we are essentially taking an inventory of our lives. But it is not a fix; it is not a syrupy self-help avenue to happiness. We do well to realize that most attempts to fix oneself can lead to fixation on oneself. Attempting to fix ourselves is inherently illogical, because it is when we become fixated on the fixing that we are led astray. There is a very big difference between operating from a self-help perspective versus taking on a reckoning of oneself. The former normally involves implementing outside principles, concepts, and practices in order to make changes in oneself, with the end goal of attaining one's own happiness. The latter has more to do with peeling away,

the relationship

layer after layer of a constructed self, so as to come into contact with the source of one's true self – God.

The reckoning process has much more to do with coming to terms with our relationship with God. It is logical for us to wonder why we should bother doing any kind of reckoning. What is in it for us? The answer: nothing and everything. Let us begin with the "nothing" side of the answer. To ask "What is in it for us?" is to assume that we are entitled to gain something for the self by going through a reckoning. It suggests that the value of enduring the reckoning process is *for us*. Otherwise, why bother? The ego loves to scream: "What's in it for *me*?" But our self-reckoning actually has little to do with us. If that is true, why on earth would we make an effort – for whom? Others? God? "Who cares!" cries the ego. But if we *really* listen to our ego crying out, what we will hear, even if only faintly, is the emptiness in that cry. It is a desperate longing to matter mixed with a defiant assertion of power – the power to shut down any and all attempts for any other revelation than the ego's truth, because if any other truth is revealed, the ego loses its standing.

Let us now turn to the "everything" side of the answer to the question "What is in it for us?". When the human ego relinquishes, to whom/what is it relinquishing? And, once relinquished, what is left behind? The "death" of the ego suggests that some other form of life replaces it. This is where the ego becomes exceedingly uncomfortable. For it to fight as hard as it does, it must be fighting from a fear of *something greater than itself*. No warrior huffs and puffs without reason – there has to be some perceived threat, if not a credible threat. What could threaten the ego? Other egos? Temporarily, yes, but inherent in the human ego is a comparative survival instinct, thus any one ego can compare itself to another and find some way to overpower it; or it can wallow in self-pity to lock in and retain the self's dependence upon its own ego for comfort. Not only does the ego huff and puff, it also moans and groans (effectively binding the person to self). The only indefatigable threat the human ego fears is God. To be clear: it is a *perceived* threat, in that the ego falsely believes it will be destroyed completely by God, but that is not the case. The ego will be transformed, not eradicated. Its beneficial functions (to itself and others) will survive and thrive in the relationship with God.

The relationship is essentially an assimilation process. God assimilates our being; our being assimilates Him (we do not *become* Him). The *only* relationship that has zero gaps is the relationship with God. The only lasting relationship is the one that cannot be broken. We can only know our trajectory when we bind ourselves to truth. We have no recourse elsewhere, no compunction to carry. Think of it this way: if lack of belief in God contains some intrinsic, sustainable abundance, then why are signs of that abundance not overpowering all the scarcity in the world, the majority of which is derived from human greed and selfishness? If we think so highly of our own abilities, how can we reconcile the vulnerability of our mere existence? Anything human made is ultimately void of lasting meaning. We are creatures and thus cannot be truth. Only God is truth. We keep trying to control the narrative of what is sacred and profane. We rely on what we think is a bullet proof identity (self), and then bleed out from the very identity that is bound to fail us, by virtue of its limitations. The deepest shame of the human ego is the false self's audacity in its vain (and in vain)

the relationship

attempt to appropriate God's ability to be God.

Unless we choose to surrender to God's will, we will always be attempting to assert self above divinity. The self is blessed with the choice to act as God's agent, not adversary. During a reckoning, the last vestiges of patterned bad behaviors and choices will hang on, desperate to survive. I held tightly to my notion that expanding my horizons by any means available was a healthy thing to do and that there would be no harm in it. Wrong. Everything fell short or became dangerous, and left me permanently parched, tormentingly hungry. The human round-and-round-we-go pattern gets old. But in letting go of self, we seek the everything. When we live by gradation, peeling away the layers of delusion, we find the connective tissue that will never be torn. We can take comfort knowing that reckoning unravels us, revealing the true self, the self we never could have imagined. Hidden in plain sight is our lasting liberation, the exponential relief of our own systematic disappearance.

The relationship with God is *the* relationship of our lives. That said, having belief in God and living belief in God are not one in the same. Therefore, a question well worth pondering:

What is my relationship with the relationship?

Chapter Six ~ Faith †

> *"...Amen, I say to you, if you have faith the size of a mustard seed, you will say to this mountain, 'Move from here to there,' and it will move. Nothing will be impossible for you."*
>
> ~ *MT 17:20*

    Imagine yourself in the minuscule as the entirety. Your every cell is fortified by a faith propensity. Holy by creation, you have everything you need. Faith, the love bound virtue, elasticizes your soul. You trust that God instilled in you an instinctual seeking of Him, a granule of His beyond infinity, with which you can move mountains. By the waters of Baptism, faith pronounces itself, bursting forth the proclamation of salvation through Jesus Christ. The proclamation, your soul's first words, are received before ever spoken or heard, for God is not dependent on your readiness to receive and listen. Your love for God is truth sealed; love's truth is that truth is love. And you will never be bound to need of evidence or proof. Believing is seeing. You are invested.

    In the relationship, one way we come to know our true self is through our faith in God. The proclamation nourishes our faith and, in spiritual gestation, we wait for the manifestation of new life, the divine life that saves. God calls us deeply into Him, and with such mystery. For Christians, by our faith we commit ourselves to God. We claim Jesus as the way, truth, and life, thereby claiming our own way, truth, and life in the Father. Through the Holy Spirit, we become an extension of the manifestation of divine love. Faith and belief are not simply mechanisms for activating our love of God; they are our love of God itself, activating us in the relationship. Faith does not create the relationship; the relationship creates faith.

Faith is the sticking point for those who do not believe or those who are unwilling to trust that God has a plan. Even the verbiage sounds awkward and creates discomfort. Nonbelievers often use the gift of human reason for the sake of *finding* truth, rather than *loving* truth. But it is not the job of faith to explain God; God can explain Himself. Human reason will create a constant state of interruption, bombarding the intellect with doubts about the veracity of faith. It is easy, for example, for the mind to dismiss Biblical accounts as being beyond the scope of possibility, much less credibility. Many view people of faith as being naive, if not delusional and duped by religious institutions. Being attached to reason is understandable, given it is something we utilize on a daily basis. Actually, it is logical to think that, by reason alone, we can move mountains (consider how humanity has used reason to accomplish all kinds of amazing feats). Reason is a gift from God and He wants us to implement it to explore, achieve, and accomplish. But reason is not the exclusive property of the relativistic or secular mind. In fact, it is by reason that we understand faith for what it is. Reason is not the enemy of faith; it is its defender. But reason without faith is unreasonable, for the most reasonable quest we make is seeking our source.

It is also not uncommon for those who doubt God to envy (perhaps secretly) those with faith, because they see how faith gets people through the seemingly nonsensical, tough times and tragedies. Likewise, with reason alone, death is a dead end reality. Thus, even if one holds dear the gift of life, the gift has an expiration date. Faith has no such end. Faith is all encompassing, as it is our spiritual gestation, life, and culmination. Yet, we who live by faith sometimes underestimate God's faith in us. If Jesus states that we only need a mustard seed's worth of faith to move mountains, who are we to deny the magnitude of His gift? No matter how far removed one might be from faith, God is not the one doing the removing. Why would God want to deny any creature its divine design? Why would God reorient the purpose for which He endowed us with faith? Our chosen propensity to live in sin and lack of integrity creeps into every aspect of our lives. And, no matter how loud we cry out, reasoning our way into giving in to temptation, the spiritual echo chamber we enter whenever we deny faith maintains an interior clamor, as we drag our way in chains.

Even for believers, faith can be one of the most challenging aspects in the relationship. This is one reason why the relationship flourishes inside the structure of religion. When I returned to the Church, I came to understand that faith is not limited to any individual's relationship with God. Faith is the binding agent in the structure of religion, joining all of us to God. In Catholicism, faith unifies the individual *and* the collective "Body" of the faithful to Jesus Christ. Each and every Catholic shares in this mystical connection (whether they

the relationship

are aware of it or not). Thus, each individual relationship with God is as important as everyone else's *and* as the totality of the relationships in the Church. Jesus deemed the individual relationship and the collective relationship with God as one when He built His Church upon the rock of the apostle, Peter. Had He merely assembled stones in order to build a physical structure, there would be "no room at the inn" for the relationship. The intricacies of faith surprised me when I returned to the Church. For so long, I had held onto the idea that faith was somehow a slippery slope to farce, delusion. It was I who was naive in my thinking. It is well worth delving into the subject of faith as it is explained by Catholicism or your particular denomination. And, if you are not a person of faith, it is beneficial to ponder if the richness of the dynamic of faith in the relationship with God is a missing ingredient in your relationships with yourself and others.

Yet, even if we are deeply embedded in our faith, there is an inherent fragility if we fall into believing that we can maintain our faith all on our own. Paradoxically, our faith cannot reach its fullness by our own accord. Faith is a God-fulfilling prophecy – a gift God initiates and activates according to His will. Our will plays an important role, in that we choose to live by faith. But our choice alone cannot sustain our faith. Receiving the Eucharist during Mass is an example of this dynamic. While it is we who must make the choice to come to the table to be nourished, our act of eating itself is not what feeds our faith. In other words, the ritual alone would be merely symbolic, were it not for the manifestation of the living Christ entering our being. Faith feeds faith. The more we are nourished by our propensity, the more we grow in the spiritual prosperity of the relationship.

book one

    The realization that there is no self without God can manifest as paralysis to the soul. It is reasonable then to understand why the ego raises a shield to block incoming expressions of faith. Perhaps, for example, some readers will be put off anytime I refer to Catholicism or Christianity. But by logic, why would any of us view another's faith (in God or no God) as a threat? Put another way, should not a self-reliant self understand what it means to live by faith, by virtue of the fact that it puts all its faith in itself?

Chapter Seven ~ Condition Critical †

So why all the fuss? Why do people get so bent out of shape where God and religion are concerned? Why all the defensiveness? Why the need to convince or refute? Why do we wince when others preach to us about religion, but then in the next breath we preach our agendas to them? Why has it become so difficult to have lively, respectful dialogue about faith? It is no surprise that any book about God is at risk of coming across as preachy. But, since God is love, were we to consider this to be a book about love, would preachy be a word we would use to describe it?

It is easy to equate emotionally charged preaching with force feeding and be repelled by it. But are negative reactions really necessary? When writing this book, for example, I could feel the walls closing in on every sentence. I wondered how any book about God can thrive within the confines of incessant human criticism. Surely readers who live their lives according to a predominantly secular ideology would denigrate anything an author might write about God. Better yet, how can pages turn on a closed book – would they not avoid such a book altogether? It dawned on me that the same negativity that fosters ongoing criticism of others, also permeates human reasoning, thus the knee-jerk devaluation of anything about God that is beyond our understanding.

If each of us were to mark down in a day a notch for

every time we had a critical thought or word (about ourselves and others), we would likely far exceed the amount of notches we could mark down for every thought and word of praise we extend to ourselves and others. Sadly, most of us live unaware of how habitually critical we are. Humanity collectively seems to have fallen into perpetual critical condition. Much of our criticism is rooted in insecurities, competitive tendencies, past hurts, and unresolved childhood upsets. In this world of opinions gone wild, our actions are often based on our fear of being criticized and/or our need to be praised. Yet, as much as we yearn for praise, we are often too stingy to offer it to others. Instead we seem to believe (even if only silently) that the more we tear down others, the easier it is to uplift ourselves. Secular society thrives on individualism; ironically, secular individualism is highly dependent upon the approval and recognition of others.

We are conditioned to condition in our relationships – to set terms and keep score, pivoting towards praise and evading criticism by controlling and rerouting relationships accordingly. Logical – praise feels good and criticism stings. Sure, we can make a 180 degrees turn and consider the "every child gets a trophy" solution to the human condition of being critical. But this approach, while well intended, encourages the falsehood that life is fair. Healthy competition and constructive criticism are useful; they encourage us to improve and motivate us to work harder, to be better. But how can we extrapolate healthy criticism in the current climate of accepted (and expected) rudeness, gossiping, finger pointing, and name calling? Consider how the platform of the Internet has turned criticism into a sport.

Criticism is married to hypocrisy, another toxic

the relationship

dynamic in human relationships. We are rife with contradictions, in our thoughts, words, and actions. Yet, even while struggling with our own contradictions, we do not cease judging others for theirs. Hypocrisy breeds disappointment. In truth, we will often be disappointed, by both ourselves and others. The worst disappointments come when our expectations are unrealistically high. The best way to face the hypocrisy of others is by first admitting to our own. We too will disappoint others, thus we would be wise to confront the reality of our own deficiencies in relationships. If we refuse to do so, we are accepting a lifetime of blame.

The dynamics of criticism and hypocrisy have no standing in the relationship with God. God's *only* condition is perpetual, unconditional love. This is such an abstract notion that it can result in our developing a state of mistrust of God. It becomes easy to adopt the popular narrative of judging God and declaring Him a hypocrite for allowing human suffering. But the notion of blame itself is short sighted, in that it adheres us to the dynamic of doom, because the other side of blame is shame. If we are blaming another for some bad behavior, it is often a way of over-compensating, so that we do not have to face the shame of our own contradictions and deficiencies. The shame we carry is the same shame we attempt to bury. Sadly, by blaming God for pain and suffering, we fail to grasp the great mystery: that God makes goodness out of everything. While on the surface it may appear that God is sometimes letting us down, God cannot disappoint in the relationship, *and* our human propensity to disappoint is nullified by His mercy. In the relationship we are always remade "*in His image and likeness.*" But, because we cannot see the goodness manifested in the whole design, we fixate on the suffering in the partial, and assume it will never be reconciled. It is easy, for example, to latch onto the narrative that religion is responsible for much of the violence in the world, (as though secularism and relativism have brought us any closer to peace and love). It is even easier to become a mouthpiece for harmony, like the beauty pageant contestant who just wants "world peace." Instead of playing the blame game, we would do better to see even a smidgen of our own tainted countenance in the most evil of faces, so that we can understand evil as just that – a reflection that tricks the eye into believing in a permanence more powerful than God's mercy.

Worthwhile questions to ponder: "Am I going to narrow my life to my ego's interests by prioritizing engaging in destructive dynamics in human relationships? Or, am I going to elevate my life by prioritizing my relationship with God?" Consider that, as the reader of this book, you do not have to bind yourself to defensiveness or criticism in order to retain whatever beliefs you have about God. This book may or may not influence your relationship with God. My primary hope is that you will consider that writing and reading a book about the relationship with God is not a human to human endeavor. You and I are not detached observers of the relationship; rather, reader and writer connect to navigate the intimacy of it. The reward is liberation from the confines of intellects and opinions. The human person is truly able to roam freely, to shake off the dust, to be bathed in refreshingly lovely light in the relationship.

Why would the Descriptionless create limited describers? God is big enough for all parts of you and me. The challenge, therefore, is to be big enough for God. As

the relationship

the writer, my thoughts and statements are not tangled up by the need to prove I am right, because I cannot help but be both right and wrong (a.k.a. human). You and I are in a process of creation in the relationship. God is creating through us both in this book; He creates through each of us *and* all of us *in everything*. In the relationship, criticism is nothing more than a sheer curtain, billowing between inside and outside realities. We can see through it, but the attraction of the sheen of criticism keeps us mesmerized, our eyes ever straining to see more clearly. We can bring to bear all the criticism we can muster, but we deprive ourselves if we stifle that which God creates through each of us individually, and all of us together. Since love is His everlasting domain, it makes sense to let Him do the creating.

Relativism is a logical position. In an expanding universe, would we not naturally want to multiply and expand self as our point of reference? All kinds and types of people coexist: tribes, nationalities, genders, races, cultures, and religions. But each of us is *uniquely and equally* relevant to God. If we morph the relative self into an absolute self, there is no room for God. The ego benefits whenever we become ensnared in a web of defensive posturing and criticizing others for their relationships with God. But if we think about it – even from a strictly evolutionary point of view, it would be illogical for us to adapt only to human relationships, because in them we will forever remain *only human*. In the relationship with God, we rise above evolutionary limitations such as "survival of the fittest." We are all fit to survive and thrive in our life with God. We are all biologically and instinctively suited for salvation.

In Part Two we will explore some of the primary dynamics God manifests in the relationship. In them, we traverse transformation. One of the most mysterious aspects of these dynamics is the way in which they form a shared experience with others within the relationship with God. When I returned to the Catholic Church, I began to notice a commonality in the ways in which people talked about and lived their faith. I wondered how it could be that the same dynamics I was experiencing *prior* to becoming educated in Church teachings, could be so accurately mirrored by others' relationships with God. People I had never met were speaking a language that was entirely organic to my relationship with God. But it was well beyond a shared faith or belief system. There was a startling familiarity, not just a sharing of ideas and practices with like-minded people. Rather, God's presence imbued in them was catching my attention. I was made aware that they are in a *living* relationship with God; His truth is *living* in them. That fusion of other and same is the binding agent. It was as though a gigantic jigsaw puzzle had been thrown into the sky and all the pieces were connecting and falling into place in perfection. But because God had prompted me to experience these dynamics *before* learning about them academically, I was able to discern in myself, and recognize in others, a visceral knowing that the relationship is, indeed, living.

I am not a theologian, thus I can only present these dynamics in a generalized way. When I began to really study Church teachings, I was flummoxed by my own ignorance and my many inaccurate opinions about Catholicism. The depth and beauty with which the Church extrapolates the dynamics in the relationship is truly staggering. Likewise the plethora of brilliant minds

the relationship

who influenced the Church throughout the ages is inexhaustible. If you want a taste of what I am referring to, peruse a document called *"Compendium of the Social Doctrine of the Church"* (a compilation of the Church's teachings on social justice). I mention this document because it is the most blatant example of how close believers and non-believers are when it comes to envisioning a peaceful world, one in which every person truly matters.

For our purposes here, when reading part two there is no need to concern yourself with intellectual understanding, or making comparisons, or defending whatever you believe. As counter-intuitive as this might sound, understanding and accepting the dynamics of the relationship is the same as questioning and doubting them. It is only when we detach ourselves from our need to know, that we truly arrive in knowing. That which is sacred holds its own.

Part 2

Sacred Dynamics

Chapter Eight ~ Initiation †

By far the most radical aspect of the relationship for me was a growing awareness that befell me that I was not the one initiating it; God was initiating all my questions and doubts and difficulties. And He had begun doing so years prior to what I had first deemed the beginning. It was unnerving to realize that I was not at the helm of my own personal inventory process. The self is always ready to take credit, thus in my habitual way I assumed that it was I who was bravely asking the tough questions. When I realized that He had been initiating from the get go, I came into an awareness of the relationship that completely reoriented me. No longer was I dismissive of or confined by any belief or structure. No longer could I superimpose anything that would come close to what I was now experiencing. A kind of unity and genuine communication manifested. My every thought of Him would almost immediately be reaffirmed as I moved through my days. I became aware of His palpable, constant presence integrating my living into my being, and my being into my living.

God initiated the relationship before He created each of us. That is an abstract notion, but think of a time when you first had a vision of something and then went about the work of creating it. That vision was you initiating a future creation. In each individual, God initiates the relationship in a way that is entirely customized to that individual. God "calls us each by name." Certainly, patterns emerge throughout humanity. For example, many of the saints lived lives that were not so saintly, but God initiated through their shortcomings. God's main vehicle for initiating in the relationship is longing. He places within each of us a deep longing for Him and induces us tenderly and consistently to move through that longing, ever deeper into Him.

One of the key factors in our longing is all the passion with which we struggle and by which we are motivated, driven. God reaches into our passion and initiates our desire for intimacy with Him. We cannot create a passion for the intimacy of the relationship on our own. It is already embedded into our hearts by God, and it is ours to discover by way of His initiation. He wants us to know it, to live it, but not as some superficial fervor. He wants us to feel it rushing in our blood, quivering our sinews and bones. He wants our voices to quake with it every time we speak and sing. It is a passion and intimacy that is so enormous we cannot contain it. God wants nothing more than for us to say such a resounding "Yes!" to Him that He can echo our deepest desire for Him and return it through His deepest desire for us. His is a love perpetually initiating and He instills in us the passion to crave it to such a degree that, until we can say "Yes!" to Him, we are saying "No!" to our life potential.

It is easy for us to get tangled in the idea that living for God means having to sacrifice our deepest desires. But God created us with desire – and our deepest desire is for Him. The self has a very different agenda in terms of desire – it redirects desire to acquire and gain control of what it wants. Living in the passion of the relationship takes us beyond a narrow definition of emotional passions and into a rich understanding of our capacity to live in true passion. We begin to fall madly in love with God by embracing the truth that He is initiating the relationship and is opening our hearts to be filled with His love. Not surprisingly, our biggest obstacle is that we very likely have fallen madly in love with self. There is plenty of room for love of self and love of God to coexist, but the ego is not on board with that plan. But if we apply basic logic, it is easy to see that the ego's agenda of love of self is short-sighted.

Imagine yourself at a point in your life where you realize that you have accomplishments, wonderful relationships, and the creature comforts you need and desire. Still, something is missing, and you do not know what it is. You quiet yourself, cease occupying your mind with distractions, and you listen. At some point you begin to wonder if this longing, this ache, this unhappiness is coming from within you. If it is, then should you not be able to fix it? And if it is not, from whence does it come? You confide in a friend or family member, you write in a journal, maybe even start seeing a therapist. But all you are able to do is unravel and expose infinite layers of this absence, this vacancy in the deeper regions of your being. So you are now very aware of the hollowness, but are helpless to remedy it. Nothing inside or outside you is able to resolve it. But then you begin to realize that, if nothing in you or in the world is at the helm or can fix it, who is and who can? What is the source of this longing, this ache etched on the heart? If the source is God, why would you not redirect your life towards Him and acquiesce your will to His? Why carry on this charade, pretending you can resolve the longing yourself? Why not go ahead and surrender? Easier said than done.

the relationship

Even when we tell ourselves that surrendering to God's will is what is best for us, we still have habitual reactions to force our own. The best way to put God back into the equation is to let Him do the talking – *listen* for what He wants of you. The direct line of communication between God and each of us has always been open. When we speak to anyone, we are speaking to God, in that our internal dialogue with Him is still present and active in all our human words and conversations, just like it is in prayer. Think of what it means to have the ability to *create* a relationship. Now think of what it means for God to have created all the people who go on to create all the relationships. *The* relationship encompasses all of this, as well as the personal relationship He shares with each of us individually. That is the abundance in which we are invited to reside.

The spiritual survival instinct is initiated by God, not by us. God placed it in us – not the reverse. Put another way, as Creator, God's every creation is His Self-Revelation initiation. We would have *no predisposition to respond* to the longing, were we not created from within His love. If you could blast open your limited self, access the fullness of your being – in mind, heart, soul, body – why would you *not* risk everything to gain everything? Because we are constantly preoccupied with so much choosing in our lives, we miss the key point: we are chosen. This seems too passive to us and we worry we have no control here. The myth of unabashed self-reliance secular society encourages us to buy into imprisons the best freedom we could ever experience: the *freedom* to surrender to God, to choose our chosen-ness. God is our winning lottery ticket, yet often we are hesitant or unwilling to gamble with the currency of faith. Instead we invest ourselves in the ongoing folly of idolizing the self. We seek the comfort of flattened dimensions in our lives because they are familiar and seemingly safe. The "everything that you want" the "all that life can be" resonates within your heart in a place so sincere that it can feel secretive, hidden, out of your reach. Out of your reach – perhaps. Out of God's reach – never. The peace of Christ lies beside us each night as we fall asleep. All memories of the darker day diffuse. He closes our eyes with the hands of His mercy, runs His fingers through our hair to blissfully comfort us. What God is doing in us keeps growing and will forever be moving in us. This train has left the station.

The beginning of humility comes when we reorient ourselves regarding initiation. God's will is not something we simply aim towards or agree to do. It is more about allowing Him to enter every part of us and choosing to surrender to the momentum of His initiation. It is a change of mind, heart, and being, wherein subtle dimensions of softness glide into us the internal movement of the Divine. Every feeling, every sensation is its own existence and is not of us but is *through* us from God. All our creations are God's creations, living inside us and being expressed through our living. The self will rebel – count on it. We are not used to this kind of "knowing." It reaches far beyond knowing by way of logic, reason, and experience. As an example, I am not sure how I could write about anything in this book if I did not "know" it in some way. But I cannot adequately describe how I "know" it. Likewise, God, the initiator of the relationship, has you here reading. I have absolutely no sway over any reader. If you are here, it is not because of me; nor am I here because of you. God's pursuit of each of us in the relationship has led us both here.

the relationship

Even the most open-minded person will fall prey to the self habitually thinking it has to *try* to be in the relationship, to *try* to follow God's will. The ego is invested in our failure in the relationship (in order to keep us dependent on the self). But, in truth, it is God Who makes us ready to follow His will, in gradations *and* all at once (simultaneously). Everything – every interaction, relationship, experience, is God-initiated and becomes one more avenue for seeking Him, pursuing Him. Our entire existence is animated by Him. In God's persistent pursuit, his ever-present love and mercy are ours to receive. He never leaves us, even when we cannot feel Him in our midst. Like cells regenerating, He is constantly initiating in us the deep desire to pursue Him with intensity. Do not hesitate to demand answers from God, to be insistent, consistent in your pursuit of Him. This dynamic of pursuit is helpful, especially during hardships. We may also experience times of dryness, as though nothing is really happening or improving. We might even fear He has abandoned us. But, as Creator, He is always in us and we remain always in Him.

The clarity of existence rests in both its separations and unifications. Initiation into the concurrent emptiness and fullness is one of the primary dynamics operating in the relationship. We can be aware of it whenever we like. Christ emptied Himself to become a servant. He became human, even though He is God. This *Kenosis*, His docile, nonresistant, obedient, humble submission to His Father's will is ours to imitate in the relationship. We are safe and can relinquish custody of our orphaned self. God's providence initiates and guides the steady flow of our truest self, the self that was made for pursuing and praising Him.

If we remain attached to self, we live our entire lives in clothes that do not really fit. Our longing for God is such that our mortal self becomes like a heavy coat, weighing down upon us over time as the body shrinks with age. God's pursuit of me brought forth a tidal wave of longing for Him. That longing has taken me full circle, into a deeper level of surrender. It strikes me that, until we realize that God is the Initiator in the relationship, we fly solo, searching for holiness in the middle of awfulness, always coming up short regarding our place in the world. We are left thirsting for a love we cannot live, until we are graced with the awareness that is has always been and will always be ours to receive. The guarantee God gives us by way of initiation is His limitless love embedded in our longing. In other words, just as each moment of time contains all moments of time, just as each moment of God's love contains all moments of God's love, our longing, too, is rendered unquantifiable because it is *already* liberated through the Risen Christ and is therefore already everlasting. Initiation becomes culmination, reverberating birth. The soul returns to the home it never left.

God's initiation is His invitation. As one invited, if I enter as a person taking, I reduce my ability to receive. If I enter wearing the incorrect "attire" in my heart and actions, I insult His inviting Spirit. It is a gift to be invited. But God does not halt the relationship at initiation; His generosity expands as He draws us ever closer, magnetizing His initiation to our conversion.

Chapter Nine ~ Conversion †

God's initiation and our conversion are concurrent dynamics in the relationship; He is the source of both. So why do we often feel uncomfortable in situations where others are expressing their religious beliefs? Why would the ego freak out and shun such people? Surely they mean well, albeit perhaps in an irritating way. Likely we resist because it is a human-to-human interaction, and is thus a limited expression of passion for God. Stated another way, it is a battle of human agendas: "I don't believe in God, so quit trying to make me" versus "I believe in God, thus you should too if you want to be saved." Or something to that affect. And then there are the slogans. The excitement of even one moment of conversion can lead to an onslaught of clichés, that often result in a concoction of some sort of verbal repellent. While it is understandable that conversion would encourage a kind of over-the-top enthusiasm, for those who have never registered conversion moments or experiences, the enthusiasm can create discomfort. It often comes across as insulting, offensive, demeaning and can make us feel violated – as though our privacy and dignity are being challenged.

Inherent in both the initiation and conversion dynamics of the relationship is a plea God instills in us, that we then resonate by way of our longing for Him so that He can move into us deeply. That plea cries: "Make me bigger than I am, Lord." We do not want to be confined by our own limitations, once we understand how much more we can be in the relationship. The relationship is not only our life with God here on earth, but also our segue into everlasting life with God in Heaven (the state of remaining forever united with Him). Conversion prompts us to say: "Lord, let me be all Yours, only Yours." Regardless if we are aware of it or not, our longing for God unites us with His initiation of the relationship, and conversion follows. Often conversion is associated with some kind of epiphany, and it can be experienced as such. It can also be slow, methodical, even painful. Regardless of its impact at any given time, we can rest assured that conversion is a continuity, not a finality. Thus, even if we experience what *feels* like the absence of God (those spaces in between conversion experiences), our conversion, nonetheless, is always moving us forward in the relationship. Maintaining this indispensable trust nurtures our faith to flourish.

The distinction between initiation and conversion is sometimes difficult to extrapolate. Initiation comes from God, stirs within us and leads to conversion. Conversion also comes from God and is a kind of internal shift. The shift might be abrupt, as tectonic plates that, after centuries of sliding in a constant state of tension, release as one slides free from the other and the earth quakes. Or the shift can be subtle and full of nuance, quiet as morning dew settling on the grass. Essentially, conversion is our response to God's initiation. But what is most liberating about it is that we can accept or decline. We are motivated by an internal shift from within the dynamic of a divine exchange, and we are blessed with the option to choose it.

the relationship

The truth about conversion is that we never know when, where, or how it might arrive. We might assume that it will be a clear, forceful sign from God of His love for us. But it can also manifest as a realization of our love for Him. Notice that love is the common agent. Early on in my conversion, I stumbled onto a youtube video of a prayer by Saint Ignatius of Loyola. The video had beautiful imagery of all aspects of creation with which God graces us, but that was not what got me. An image of a secluded beach and placid sea emerged on the screen. And then the text: "I am standing before God, our Lord" followed by the first line of a prayer: "Take Lord and receive..." Somehow, the purity and sincerity of that expression of love *for* God produced a palpable shift in my being. It was far beyond the sensation of being emotionally moved by the words; I was transformed by them. It was as if a purified but deeply buried love opened my heart. Conversion by youtube...who knew!

God has initiated in us a curiosity about him, one that has been part of us even before we were conceived. He then chooses when and how to shape us. And that shaping can take on all kinds of interesting methods of conversion. This is why I am able to write and you are able to read about conversion, regardless if we practice the same religion or belief system. At its most basic, the relationship is a simple exchange – between each of us and God. And every one of these exchanges – past, present, and future – was designed by the Creator. God holds it all together. The whole is woven and interconnected, beyond time and space, remaining entirely inclusive. A perfect moment, one in which you are everything else and everything else is you, is both vanishing and eternal. There is a locked-in, beyond time and space quality. And God steers all of us on a steady course by His love.

Conversion does not need a political campaign, full of slogans and false promises. Jesus was never a politician. He willingly shared parables and teachings without imposing rigid interpretations. The Lord's Prayer is recited as He taught us to pray. His living Word permeates every part of our being; it is not confined to our ability to parrot scripture passages. If we hold fast to a flat interpretation of conversion, we may be spouting off slogans to convince ourselves more than others. God speaks to each of us uniquely, in a way that only we can hear and understand; should we not trust He will do the same with others? We would do well to distinguish the difference between force feeding God to others versus spreading seeds that others can choose to sow or not to sow. This does not mean we must abandon our convictions or passion; it simply means we should not be attached to any outcome.

The self will naturally try to appropriate conversion. But, in reality, there is nothing any of us can do to get there; *only* God can bring each of us to Him in a way that allows us to become the person He created us to be. It is God Who renders conversion an everlasting dynamic in the relationship. Thus all of our "trying to become" is just us chasing our own tail like some wound up, crazy hound. We spin round and round within our thoughts, emotions, and perceptions about God. As limited beings, we cannot sustain all of Him in ourselves, yet rest assured He does sustain all of us in Him.

the relationship

The Gift of You

If you could take all your moments, those of fear, anxiety, pain, joy, laughter, longing, and all your gifts and experiences and then place every aspect of yourself, condensed into one moment of time, you would see yourself the way God sees you – as a totality of being, a perfect oneness, entirely equal to all others, in that each person's totality is locked in the same perpetual moment that yours is. This is, perhaps, what it must be like to exist in God's time – no beginning or end, no consecutive or concurrent, no and, no or. The more you defer your "you" to God, the more abundant and fruitful your life becomes. Suddenly and slowly your being opens like a flower, basking in warmth and radiance. In your oneness, you get to perceive yourself as an entity that functions with equal measure – meaning what you used to see as your "negatives and positives" now both become essential to your all, to the totality of you. And that totality, once offered to God, moves from the scarcity of self-to self, into the abundance of God-to self.

You may be wondering: "Conversion – to what?" If you are the one who decides it, it is not true conversion. This does not mean you play no role in it; but it does mean you do not initiate it or define it. True conversion means you cannot *help* but to be converted. For example, imagine yourself in some beautiful place in nature, alone with your thoughts and emotions, when something moves inside you. You cannot put your finger on it, but you know you are being taken somewhere — into a quietness, a state of being where you could never take yourself. That is the movement of the Holy Spirit. Your *entire* life is an opening for God. And the perfection God brings opens your totality. Conversion is both the expansion of self and self actualization. In it, you come to know, without a doubt, that you could never experience the entirety of your self through yourself or through anything outside yourself. Only God can realize your perfection. God has "called you by name." God has saved you in particular. God loves you in totality, not in parceled out bits of love.

Moving through the murky darkness of human living, we arrive in the place where we can become closest to God and reveal ourselves completely and still be loved. When we let ourselves go there with Him, His light begins to glow in our hearts and souls. We are welcomed with an open heart into a new intimacy. The most genuine and profound of all intimate relationships is *the* relationship. In this one relationship, we find everything we need. It does not necessarily feel this way, especially at first. Challenges continue to arise and our longings linger. But all longing takes on a new meaning. The hunger in the relationship now becomes connected to our insatiable desire for the truth – that we are intimately loved and that our entire existence in God is enough.

Conversion Challenges

One struggle that can emerge is related to our need for overt signs, big moments of conversion and direct, supernatural experiences of God. Even if we have such an experience (called a "theophany" in Catholicism), a kind of depression can follow because we are now acutely aware of our limited human self, thus we see our lives from within that limitation and can have a very hard time reconciling ourselves to it. This is a fruitful condition for

the relationship

us, because we are set on the path of seeking God's truth. He will accommodate us. The good news is that seeking and finding becomes a way of life for us. Once we reach that point of no return (to our limited self), we embark upon a journey that is so liberating that we have no qualms about losing ourselves. But we ought also be careful not to become like addicts, hooked on our private revelations or mystical experiences. The preciousness of direct experiences of God is that they remove all doubt; the risk is that they intoxicate.

Other human traits kick in to challenge us in our conversion. We might find ourselves dwelling in impatience as we wait for God to activate our purpose for His will. Our impatience is tied to our need to control time. The only thing to do is to keep reminding ourselves that His kind of time is completely outside ours, and to remain aware that every ticking moment, every inhale and exhale, are as complete as our entire lives, because His love is always entirely present. How could it not be if He is love itself? How could any human life possibly lack significance if God's will is embedded into it? How could any potential purpose a human has be rendered ineffective if that purpose is a gift from God? How can any of us reject our vocation if God is the one doing the calling? How can fear hold us back when it is the all loving, *almighty* God equipping us with the bravery and protection we will need? The intimacy of God's truth in the relationship is staggering.

Any urgency on our part to attempt to convert others might actually be an expression of scarcity – as if we do not hurry to do our part to bring others to God, we will fail God and ourselves. But only God converts others, even if He uses us as instruments in doing so. Again, if we

book one

consider God's will as the abundance in which we reside, we can see how when we engage in that abundance, all we are manifests to its fullest capacity at any given moment. We are enough, exactly as we are, and we will continue to be enough, exactly as we become. There is no reason for you to let the urgency related to chronological time fool you. You need not succumb to the idea that you are so important to God that you have to do it all before you run out of time. That said, once you have said "Yes!" to God, you will experience a quality of urgency that is very productive, for you and others. It is the urgency of having "fire in your belly," burning with love of and for God. And this you will want to share as often as possible, and from within the uniqueness of your being as a creation of God's.

When I reflect on my conversion, the one thing that stands out is that I *demanded* answers. I wanted to know the God who created me. Since I was a very lapsed Catholic, I found I had to fight (myself mostly) to return to Him. The fight of the limited self is the good fight; it prepares the soul to fight temptation and evil. Fighting evil is also the good fight; it is the right thing to do, plain and simple. When conversion is imminent, forces of destruction are most threatening. Conversion ultimately requires facing the darkness within oneself in order to bask in the light of God's love. We are forever moving towards that love, by way of both attraction and resistance. The fusion of the internal and external battles mirrors the tug of war between personal conversion and world conversion – micro and macro spiritual growth and renewal. Conversion is the battlefield where we blossom into the soldiers for Christ that we have always been. We flower in the fight. Our bounty is harvested in the relationship. What feels like waiting, wanting, longing,

the relationship

needing becomes what *is* – the present, the now of God that is soul-filling, abundant, and ours to claim.

Conversion is always a shared experience that includes unification within oneself, with God, and with others. It is a dynamic that places us on a level playing field with each other. We become aware of God's presence in our every interaction with others. And we become more aware of our sinful thoughts, words, and actions. We move softly, fluidly, unified with God, Who is love. Our longing shifts us into purified interactions with others. And we fall in love with God, over and over again.

As an integral part of creation, we spin and fall and climb and reach in the same safe space. There is nowhere to go. God begins to accelerate the constitution of our being, calling each of us into direct contact with Him. We do not just remember conversion; we continuously re-experience it. God is relating with each of us (and all of us), in each moment simultaneously. That is the fixed density of Truth. The study of God and the experience of God become one in the same in the relationship. Deep within His gift of conversion is the hidden promise that our will, will indeed convert to His. When we make time for Him, He surrenders time to us. Yet God also reminds us that time is not ours to waste. Time is the clock He sets for the sake of our souls.

Even if the self is on board regarding conversion, the likelihood that self will relinquish control of the timeline and its own agendas is slim. The ego will continue to barricade. But rest assured that surrendering to God has nothing to do with cowardice, shame, guilt, weakness, failure, or capitulation. It is about freedom, discipleship, humility. God is not taking charge of you against your will; you are using your will to receive God operating in your life. Each person's conversion story is God's will and Word amplified by the individuated heart beating in praise for Him. We are each under lock and key and cannot be the fullness of who we are without Him. He can call you through anything – love, joy, pain, and suffering. If you want to fully be yourself, spend time with God every day. He is the one who will show you to yourself. It is not about placing Him in all your relationships; it is about placing all your relationships in Him.

God woos us in the relationship, always extending the hospitality of hope. There is a spiritual *luxury* in conversion. Glide. Fall in love, like the breeze in the branches when the Spirit with the leaves dances. Following God is like floating down river with the current. Just let go. No need to fight it. Ask God to take all of you, so that you might give all to God through the person He created you to be. Conversion amplifies every human cell to resound in praise of God's constant presence. And although His mysterious and glorious plan to which we have been called to witness, serve, and honor is not ours to know until it happens, we can take comfort in knowing with certainty that we will find our true self in God's will. We are shaped in conversion as the tides, compelled by lunar magnetism, catching a glory ride on God's eternal waves.

Chapter Ten ~ Revelation †

"Truth is truth because it is truth."
~ *Romano Guardini*

Perhaps you are questioning the value of submission to God's will. You might be wondering: "Where is the fun in letting God decide my purpose and rule my life?" It is logical to question and doubt that which is inaccessible within, until it is revealed. Have you ever had a moment where truth seemed to flutter across your mind so softly, so quickly and then vanished before you could recollect or articulate it? Who exactly communicates truth in such a way? How does a truth that seems to come from outside you, so profoundly pronounce itself inside you? Perhaps it happened right as you were falling asleep, as though a thread to a dream. Perhaps it arrived through your senses, perceptions, or prayers. Intertwined in this truth is a presence far greater than we can know or imagine from within our finite minds. And the very abstractness of these experiences places us inside a kind of mystery that is at once palpable and completely beyond our reach. But this mystery, while ephemeral, is a *living* mystery. In other words, something supernatural has just been communicated to you. The Holy Spirit has just made contact. God has revealed to you a glimpse of His everything.

If you want more than a glimpse, the Bible is the best source. We directly encounter God's revelation in Sacred Scripture. It is in the Old Testament that we read about God the Father, and the Son and Holy Spirit are introduced through prophecies. The New Testament is comprised of the Gospels and reveals to us the Father's merciful sacrifice in the life, death, and Resurrection of Christ, as well as the Father and Son's gift of the Holy Spirit to mankind. Sacred Scripture comprises what we know as public revelation. This is the revelation we all share in common, thus it is the constant truth of each of our individual relationships with God *and* of our collective human relationship with God. While different faiths relate to Sacred Scripture from different interpretations and viewpoints, many believe that God is revealing His Truth from within scripture. This gives us a common ground for understanding God's revelation communication. Truth is accessible to all.

The relationship is where humanity finds its oneness, in its entirety, throughout all time. The relationship never changes because God never changes. Since God never changes, even within His mystery we have clarity of path. Because God reveals, He leads. And, as He leads, He reveals. The seeking self is in constant dialogue with the source of its pursuit (though the seeking self may be unaware of this dialogue). God reveals Himself to the seeking self and, in His revelation, God narrates the stories of every person's lifelong conversion. This is why all conversion stories, to some degree, mirror each of us to ourselves and to others. Conversion exists within the revelation of God's truth, thus saint and sinner stand on even ground. God can and does reveal His truth to each of us in unique ways in our lives. One man might find God's truth while locked in a prison cell. Another might have a

the relationship

religious vocation. The equality is fleshed out in God's love of all His creatures. It is difficult for us to believe that God can love even the most despicable person. He may not love the person's actions, but He does love the person and is always calling the person home through His mercy. The Revelation of God's love for us is the equanimity, the undercurrent of all conversion stories and witnessing of Truth.

Truth begets truth. The fullness of each self as a creation is, has been, and always will be fully at God's disposal. We are the only ones holding back in the relationship. God cannot hold back His love and truth; to do so would create a void and, as Creator, he is unity. Nothing can go missing on His watch. We, on the other hand, exist in the void of the false self to the extent that we are constantly readjusting our spiritual anatomy. For us, it is always a realignment process. Yet, each of us, at any time, can choose to let go of all futile attempts to reconstruct an identity. When we voluntarily relinquish the false self, our true self emerges because our true self is part of the 'nothing can go missing on His watch' dynamic.

Revelation poses a question to each of us: "Who do you want to be?" No human self is truth, thus no human self is God. However, God's truth is the gift that, even if hidden, is always readily available to each self within the relationship. Thus each self might do well to ask: "How do I best live my God given truth?" In this way, misguided reverence for self guides one to reclaim reverence for God. When God's truth is revealed, the *revelation itself* puts us on equal footing with Truth. God is not out to trick us about His truth. Nor will He force it upon us. The more we consent to His will, the more He reveals His truth inside the relationship. This is why simply acknowledging being in the relationship is a great first step for anyone who is seeking.

The secular self is self-perpetuating, so while the secular self is transitioning into living consciously inside the relationship with God, it will try to circumvent all revelation and reorient it to self. This is easiest for the self to do when we are disconnected from religion and instead are living in the relationship our own terms. When I returned to the Catholic Church, I had to live in the relationship in a new way – on the Church's terms this go round. Of course I immediately began to pick and choose the parts of the faith I liked and secretly dismissed the rest. The problem with that approach was that self was at the helm (though she was doing her best to pretend otherwise). Through both public and private revelation, I came to understand (albeit incrementally) that being in the relationship concurrently with being a member of the Church *exponentially* invigorated the momentum of my conversion. Why? Because the relationship is intrinsic to revelation and revelation is intrinsic to the Church. "No man is an island." The self fights this truth because it longs to maintain its identity and position of control in the relationship – to continue to have a say, to have and eat its cake. It is easy to see how counter-productive this is to the relationship. Until the self says a full and unconditional "Yes!" to God, the relationship remains lopsided. God becomes a God of convenience to a self who continues to call the shots.

Revelation reveals to us the majesty of God's love in the relationship. For billions of people who have walked and continue to walk this planet, the revealed truth is that God sent His only Son, Jesus Christ, to suffer and die for

the relationship

the forgiveness of sins, for the sake of our salvation. Just as Christ made Himself a gift for us, so too can we offer ourselves as a gift for Him, in a free and loving exchange – a divine to human, human to divine reciprocity. All our relationships flourish when we engage in them as free and loving exchanges. The most viable currency of that exchange, in all our relationships, is love. Love of God, love of one's neighbor, love of self are inextricably interconnected. The secular self actually depletes this love when the self lives disconnected from the relationship with God. Even if one has a healthy love of self and practices genuine love of one's neighbor, without the *sustaining* love of God, all other love eventually loses its luster. Loving within human limitations is limited loving. God's love knows no limitations.

The revelatory relationship is love and truth, total and pure. In this respect, no human to human relationship can ever be entirely revelatory. *Because* Jesus Christ is the Revelation, the Word Made Flesh, truth in man and God is united. Through revelation, God communicates His love for humanity. We can receive His communication by reading Sacred Scripture, attending church services, and in the subtle whispers God uses to privately reveal His love for each of us. But there is also a means by which God communicates His love to us in the relationship that is unlike *anything* we experience in human relationships. It is called grace.

Chapter Eleven ~ Grace †

God's grace is the soul's oxygen, freely endowed upon us, independent of our inhaling and exhaling. Nothing of spiritual value happens in us, to us, through us, absent God's grace. Grace is a revelatory, regenerative dynamic in the relationship. We find favor and are sanctified through God's grace. God reveals Himself to us as a loving, protective friend and ally. By way of grace, God communicates with each of us in distinctly personal ways. And it is by grace, this unmerited gift, that we are brought to salvation.

As rational creatures, we cannot elevate ourselves into the supernatural abundance that is only God's to give. Through grace, God makes us bigger than we can make ourselves. We each have people in our lives who bring out the best in us and, because of their love for us and our love for them, we are better people for knowing them. But no person can grace us with God's love, unless God's grace is operating. None of us can self-generate love outside the relationship. This does not mean that we must have an *awareness* of being in the relationship, or an affiliation with a particular religion in order to love. But it does mean that the love with which we create loving relationships with others could not happen absent God's grace. Our rational minds tend to gravitate to notions of earning, deserving, and entitlement when it comes to exchanges in our human relationships. And,

the relationship

while we often give freely, we are nonetheless attached to give-and-take standards when relating to others. God has no need of taking; everything in creation is already His. Seeking His grace, rejecting it, attachment to it, expectation of it – these are all human agendas in the relationship. Grace is so "amazing" precisely because it is removed from all constraints of human relationships. Its nature is freedom and abundance because its source is God.

You might be wondering: "Okay, so how do I *get* more of this 'amazing' grace?" It is common sense to want to acquire that which will benefit us. It can be frustrating, at first, to learn that there is nothing we can do to earn grace. But is it not a relief to realize that the Spirit of God operates freely in our lives? God's grace is always present and available. It is both a method and means by which He communicates His love for us. Experiences of God's grace are decidedly different than any other spiritual experiences. For example, when in nature and alone, it may be easy for you to register God's presence. You might even become reliant on nature to be your church – the place where you feel God. But *feeling* God, in and of itself, does not enable us to be filled with God. Through His grace, we receive the infilling of His Spirit in our very being.

I envision grace as a funnel through which God pours into me all that I need from Him – but in His time and way. What does grace actually *feel* like inside me? The closest comparison I can make is that it registers as a fusion of intuition and clarity of being. But that only scratches the surface. There is a sensation of God's movement, His presence in me, body and soul. It is as though His immeasurable energy is barely dusting my being *and* embracing all of me – simultaneously. I feel alive, but a kind of alive that I have never known before. It is not necessarily associated with a supercharged sensation or effusive emotional quality. Nor is it, for me, merely a contemplative, silent soothing. It is more like being lifted into oneself. It is subtle, yet formidable. It is as though God simultaneously lures me into it and showers it upon me. It is a humbling relief, because I at once realize how very small the self I know as me truly is – and I am so glad I no longer have to work so hard to maintain her. Grace fills me with instant understanding that all my efforting in life has been largely unnecessary, or at the very least, seriously misguided. But the most surprising reward is my *total* lack of doubt. In all my other spiritual endeavors, I was always trying to *get* something or somewhere – to some state of completeness and happiness. But I would repeatedly default to doubts about the practice, myself, my worth, my purpose. And, inevitably, I suffered a sense of profound insignificance, as though my life could come and go without me accomplishing anything worthwhile.

With grace, we are elevated beyond our waiting and hoping for some imagined degree of worth. With grace we are readied to receive. And, once received, grace creates an opening in us for more grace *to be received*. I use the passive voice intentionally, since receiving grace is not accomplished through any actions on our part. We can pray for it, but only God can dispose us to receive it. Thus, it is by grace that we are elevated beyond superficial faith. It is by grace that we are anchored in God's presence and in the awareness that *is* His abiding constancy in our entire being. It is by grace that we internalize the relationship. Grace is beyond the capacity of conscious action (since we cannot fabricate it). Hence,

the relationship

searching for grace is like trying to cup water in your hands while roaming the desert; one has no control over the spillage and evaporation. One of the biggest mysteries is when and why God chooses to endow us with grace. Hence, we benefit by consistently emptying ourselves of our will and deferring to His. Grace continuously reactivates the relationship with God and keeps it open, living, growing. Grace is the stamp of the Almighty. *Everything* hinges on grace.

The Language of Grace

God's grace is a language all its own, and part of what receiving it entails is finding a way to translate it, to oneself and to others. But realize that, if God's grace is unlike anything else, I can only get so far in translation and interpretation. I cannot speak His language to you; only He can do that. But you can take the risk and choose to open yourself and see what happens. I took that risk and can honestly say that the risk is *microscopic* when compared to the rewards. Of all of the things you do for yourself, to improve your life, none of them will ever be remotely close to how your life will change when you are on the receiving end (and beginning) of His grace. Anytime you feel yourself *trying* to receive grace, tell God you know you cannot bestow it upon yourself, because it is His and only His to give. And then listen readily and simply remain open, willing to receive.

Revelation and faith open us to grace. By grace, we are uplifted to the supernatural. While religion provides us with structure, rituals, and guidance, the relationship itself is limitless. In fact, the notion of entering into it is inaccurate. How do you "enter" a place, a state of being, a communion in which you are already an integral part? We are the habitation, the communication – because God created us. Grace opens us to choose His will. Returning to the Church, to God, to the relationship, is *always* initiated by God's grace, supported by God's love, and brought to fruition by God's will. You might wonder why God has any need for us to participate, since He can make it all happen on His own. He designed us with free will for His purposes. He casts us out in love and calls us home in love. If we dwell in feelings of rejection because we were cast out, or participate in doubting Him as a way of avoiding returning to Him, we are latching onto scarcity as a mode for living. Sin, once again, finds its foothold. Our hearts, once again, reject abundance.

God can open any of us, at any time, through any means, to receive His grace. His gift of free will is well embedded into our DNA. Returning our will to Him is the unraveling of a life-long process. It is essentially a returning that activates our ability to "regift." But this go round we are not passing along a scented candle to a friend for selfish reasons (let's face it, we regift what we do not want to keep). Receiving and then regifting God's will is directly related to receiving God's grace and regifting its impact through our words and actions. And we cannot receive or regift unless God wills us to do so. Even our good works are a byproduct of God's will. If we only help others as a way of feeding our ego and reserving our ticket to Heaven, we will fall short. Our will must be continuously relinquished to God's – completely and without conditions. We are safe to be brave, to be ready to sacrifice it all, regardless if that means we will suffer, go without, even die. When Christ died on the cross, He submitted His entire will to His Father, for our sake. When we surrender our will for His sake, we die with

the relationship

Him and are with Him saved. Opening our hearts to receiving grace is something we can take into every nook and cranny of our being and life, just as we open our lungs to receive oxygen.

Remember, if your unrelenting, indefatigable, ego-driven self is the one reading this, you will hit wall after wall, and self will likely use its veto power to stop you dead in your tracks. All you can do is to be on the lookout for its influence over you and manually override it time and again. God's grace is truly a blessing with this challenge. Every time you deny self, you rely more on Him. This pleases Him because He has so much love and mercy to give you through His grace. Once I began to surrender to God's will, fear was redefined for me. Fear usually awakens when one is threatened in any way. But God did not terrorize me with fear. He graced me with something far more powerful: wonder and awe. And I became aware that the fragility of my human life was only part of the story. Everlasting life with God is the whole story. I say God graced me with this because, until I was able to feel fear in *both* its fullness and emptiness, I was its prisoner. In the fullness of fear, I am helpless. But God overwhelms and empties all fear into His abundant love and mercy. I still have fear – often – but I now realize my fear is *graced* by God, which means it is in very good hands and, by that logic, so am I.

We are all undeserving of God's grace – not because we are sinners, but because "deserving" is not a prerequisite to something that is freely given. Even the worst sinner can be forgiven and converted by God's merciful grace. That said, accepting our inability to beckon grace and receive it at will (our will) is not easy. Without moments of grace, we might feel like we have been living in a desert during the worst drought imaginable. We seek relief, and outside inspiration offers a quick fix.

Grace is different from inspiration, though at times it may feel like inspiration. Inspiration is doubt divided. This is because in every doubt lies a glimmer of hope, and in every hope a glimmer of doubt. Thus, when we feel inspired, we are actually dividing our doubt so that we can linger in hope for awhile. This is why inspiration often fades as time passes and doubt reclaims us. We divide other aspects of self. We sin and we set aside our sins. In every sin lies the possibility for forgiveness. And, anytime we forgive ourselves when we sin, we run the risk of letting ourselves off the hook and repeating the sin. There is a barrier to break in order to extract ourselves from these entrapping dynamics. The ego is adept at overriding its contradictions and hypocrisies. Even if we are aware of them, we often opt to somehow resolve them later. We are also at risk of getting caught up solely in the *inspiration* we receive from religion, faith, and belief in God. That inspiration, though in many ways beneficial, cannot fabricate grace. We cannot survive by inspiration alone. Grace is the inspiring force of God; we are breathed into life through God's grace. This is so counter-intuitive to the secular mindset, which encourages us to continuously attempt to nourish ourselves with this artificial sweetener we call inspiration.

Because God is the source of grace, there is absolutely no mistaking grace for anything else. Grace is in alignment with truth. Unlike inspiration (doubt divided), grace unites us to God. It is a connectivity that is impossible for any human to simulate or destroy. It is so much bigger than we are. Most of us have had a moment

the relationship

(on a mountain, beach, in a meadow, looking at a rainbow) where we have had a flicker of recognition as to our tininess inside the grandeur (regardless if we attribute the grandeur to God or not). But grace stirs us in our core. It is at once outside us and permeating us entirely. It never fades, even when we are removed from the awareness or memory of it. It has no attachment to time or place. And, most importantly, we cannot help but be converted by it. It is both a starting point for conversion and continuous nourishment for our ongoing conversion.

In God's grace, all else instantly reveals itself as a lie. The only thing that now makes any organic sense is God. And, though we can relate to grace by reason, grace is independent of us; it is not a dialogue, in that we cannot respond in its language. We can only absorb it; it has no need to absorb us. And, its arrival is not constricted to a point of departure or end, because it was there all along. I do not mean to imply that grace always looks the same or has the same impact. We are each one of a kind and, as such, our Creator relates to each of us uniquely. But there is no mistaking grace, just like one could never mistake a gale for a gentle breeze. Grace is endlessly intriguing because it is simultaneously so other, yet so humanly necessary. Grace instills the presence of Christ; He takes up permanent residence in one's soul.

Grace tips the scales. Initial moments of conversion that you had not recognized until now, will become vivid, highly logical moments in your journey. By God's grace, you are restored to the self God created you to be, the self you always knew you could be. But do not breathe easy yet, for the real work of your life may be just around the bend. What will attack you next? Likely doubts, fears, temptations, laziness – all the same stuff as before. The difference is you already *are* the relationship. You always have been, but perhaps have had to seek and seek. Seeking implies becoming or acquiring. How can you become or acquire something you have been and had all along (even when you flat out rejected it)? You now know it is time for you to put forth that with which you have been blessed all these years. If you backslide into doubt and despair, no need to fret. Try to find some quiet, some stillness – through prayer or even taking a spiritual nap. Stop doing and listen. Let God lead the conversation. Let God *be* the conversation. Give Him room to respond to your doubts and questions. His grace does not evaporate – ever. It is even sewn in to the fabric of all suffering, thus if you feel separated from Him, delve into your suffering as a way of reconnecting with Him, rather than resisting it and (likely) making it worse. All must simply be offered to God. Darkness cannot consume you in His grace. Brightness will not blind you to His love (though you will likely need to squint).

It is endearingly comical how, even when grace enters by way of intense spiritual experiences, we still think we have to *do* something to cling to it, to possess it. We forever try to take the helm to steer ourselves to shore. Impossible and a waste of energy. Only God brings us safely to the shores of His mercy. God's grace sails. In it there are no coincidences. It is serendipity surrendered. One thing I notice is that, with any grace I receive, whatever insights bloom inside me show up right away in my day. For example, I will feel God's presence and be graced with some rich nugget of His truth, then it will immediately show up in ways that I could neither control nor predict (perhaps as a topic on a T.V. show, or in a conversation with a stranger, or in a book I pick up

the relationship

randomly). And, even though it at first seems to be one of those "coincidences" or "synchronicities" that happen because my mind is attuned in a particular direction, I quickly begin to realize how impossible it would be for me to have orchestrated the specificity of the moment. In the past I might have relied on Eastern religion or New Age philosophy and posited that it was "The Universe" working in my life (meaning I would have to be in a personal relationship with "The Universe"). That, then, begs the questions: "Did the Universe create itself? And did it create me?" And how can an impersonal Universe be in a personal dialogue and relationship?" I now understand the universe as the unfolding revelation God is initiating in our relationship.

Another indicator of grace operating in our lives is that certain people begin moving into our sphere. It is as though the perfect person arrives, just in time to fill a void, or solve a problem, or offer assistance. We might form relationships with some of these people, wherein we are consistently moving towards God. Or we might have short interactions that specifically draw us into the relationship with God. God graces us with people who help us become closer with Him so that we do not become isolated in our relationship with Him. He blesses us with others as the means by which to grace us with His gratitude for our willingness to seek Him.

One of the best mechanisms we can implement to better prepare ourselves to receive grace is our gratitude. Gratitude is a point of entry to God's will because we abandon our ego and give credit where all credit is due: to God. To expand our understanding of gratitude, it is helpful to reduce it to its smallest common denominator – to cultivate gratitude in the details, and hold that gratitude as equal to our gratitude for the big wins. For example, if it is God's will that, through some of the words of this book, you will be opened to God's grace, then the entire book is a win. All of us feel gratitude. For an atheist or a committed secularist, the source of that gratitude might be defined as resulting from one's actions or from luck. This is not to say that an atheist or secularist cannot possess an ongoing "attitude of gratitude." But is that "attitude of gratitude" a result of a motivational philosophy or desire to control one's own optimism? Highly motivated people tend to get things done. But motivation itself is not a God; affirmations are not the Word Made Flesh.

When all points towards self, even if it is well-intentioned and produces positive results, the dead end is inevitable. If all our gratitude is directed towards self or the notion of luck, our gratitude is *limited*. Unlimited gratitude is *only* possible when it is received from and directed towards our unlimited God. Unlimited gratitude is one way we get to witness the depth of our relationship with God. Why? Because it is a byproduct of God's incomprehensible love and mercy, rendered through His grace. When we direct our gratitude towards God, we open ourselves to receive much more than we could ever give, to ourselves, to our loved ones, to God, to anyone. *Gratitude readies us to receive the grace that readies us to give to others.*

While this chapter treats grace in a generalized way, Catholicism offers an in depth, bountiful understanding of grace (which includes a variety of types of grace and the interplay of grace, merit, and justification). But for our purposes here, think of it like this: If you had created everything and everyone, would you not want to operate

the relationship

through all of it? Is it not where you would find your fullness of expression? Place yourself in that seat just for a moment, so as to better understand why you rely on your Creator (rather than on yourself) to keep His creation going, growing, expanding. As Creator, would you not be constantly creating within creation itself? Would you not seek anyone whom you created who rejected you, ignored you, refused to accept your love? Would you not lovingly pursue that person by dispensing grace so that the person would awaken and choose you, so as to regain every ounce of love they refused?

Grace has a momentum. A living stream of love moves in your depths, regardless how much you fight it, deny it, resist it, avoid it, or refuse it. In stillness, eyes closed, feel His tremor resonating in your cells. Open to His limitlessness. Cast yourself away from fears of letting go, and embrace the courage you already possess. Any vessel must be emptied to be refilled. God appreciates it when we empty ourselves so that He can fill us with abundance and truth. Grace is the spirit of God operating – through each of us in the relationship, and simultaneously through all of us in the relationship. Every human life is an overture of His grace.

Chapter Twelve ~ The Word †

> *"In the beginning was the Word, and the Word*
> *was with God, and the Word was God.*
> *He was in the beginning with God; all things*
> *were made through Him,*
> *and without Him was not anything made*
> *that was made."*
> *~ John 1:1-3*

    I lean on the letters of these words and cannot maintain my balance. Words that mislead are often the very words that reveal, as though we must first be lost before being found. For at the heart of John's writing is the heart of the Spirit, beating a trail to truth already realized. Because Christ is the Incarnate Word, the Word made flesh, one way in which He speaks Himself into us is through Sacred Scripture. He is what He says and He says what He is. When we speak of the Word, we are in essence speaking of both The Word Made Flesh, (meaning the Logos of the Father becoming the man Christ) and Sacred Scripture (the inspired Word of God). The Word bolsters and sustains all dynamics of the relationship, individually and collectively. Thus, initiation, conversion, revelation and grace are intertwined with the Word in the relationship. Yet, it is easy to mistakenly cling to a perceived distinction

the relationship

between Sacred Scripture and the Word made Flesh. It is understandable, as this all becomes very abstract to the mind that wants clearly defined parameters and immediate comprehension.

Words that we read in books, blogs, greeting cards, letters, emails, forms, documents, advertisements, creative works – these are human words, jumbled in all different directions, guiding minds, building intellects, evoking emotions, communicating ideas, instructing, inspiring, describing, analyzing – all human domains for words. *The Word* is so radically beyond our capacities with words. It is not simply the collection of Biblical stories, Gospels, Psalms and the like. God's Word is *living*, transcendent, omniscient, eternal. It is the Incarnate Word, the Living Christ, in our midst and not just on the pages of Bibles.

If all we had was an historical account or story about the life of Christ, the Word would fall flat and we would never be able to imitate His goodness or access His grace. Scripture gives us much more than a plot line; it provides us with the evidence of truth, as well as the means of reversing our interior gravity towards sin. We get to choose faith in the revelation. We can never source ourselves or transcend our humanity via another human being. No person, past present or future, is capable of his/her own enfleshment. Christ was capable of His because He is God. In the Word, form and content are synonymous. Words reach beyond the scope of arranged letters in Sacred Scripture; they exist as particles on the page. Think of Jesus, sinless, in the flesh, performing miracles and initiating a stream of followers that winds all the way back to Adam and Eve, as well as forward to the culmination of humanity and beyond. We are made from the Incarnate Word. By the Word, we are forever in the relationship with God. The Word is audible to the human soul. Through the Word, we make contact with the Creator. In the Word, God makes contact with us. With the Word, the Holy Trinity remains ever and always present, in communication with us. If we were able to scatter into space all letters from all alphabets, all words from all languages – from all eras past present and future, we still would only be using these as entry points into and tools for access to the Word. Stated another way: the Word is not confined by the material words in the Bible. We know this best because our relationship with Christ, the Word made flesh, is not solely reliant upon our reading and interpretation of the Word in Sacred Scripture.

If we think of Jesus Christ, dying on the cross for all human sin, we do not think of all human sin as defining Jesus Christ. The Word is the living death and the death living. On the faith plain, death is a passing wind, a tumble weed scurrying its way across the arid land. Below the faith plain, death is a wicked sorrow, finite, unconquerable. The Word is the elevation of death. The Word Made flesh is the parameter-less, timeless, manifestation of the love and mercy of God. Thus, every time we nourish ourselves with the Word by way of reading Sacred Scripture, we are in direct access to this love and mercy. Yet, were we to memorize the entire Bible, we could never *possess* the Word. There would never be a need for us to do so. When we access God's love and mercy, we do not pocket it, take it home and retrieve it later. Our access to love and mercy through the Word is present, constant, and everlasting. We are merely limited in our ability to experience it as such.

the relationship

I used to read scripture with the desire to decipher it, to extract its melodies and mysteries. Eventually I began to enter into the Word in a different way (and not by my own doing). Through grace, my being was prompted to retrieve the Word and extricate it from my flat, lackluster prior ways of reading it. As the Word became authentically alive in me, I became authentically alive in it. But I could have never decoded it myself. In fact, the only code that got in the way was my own narrow translation. Eventually I came to read it plain as day, without laboring to understand it or explain it or recite it or study it. Therein lies the mystical union we each have with the Word, regardless if we realize we have it or not. To be clear, this does *not* mean that we become the Word, or that through the Word we arrive at a state of being on equal terms with God. Rather, mystical union with the Word is a deeper relationship to the Word, thereby amplifying our relationship with God. Just as we grow in intimacy with loved ones by communicating our thoughts and feelings, so too do we grow in intimacy with God when we open ourselves to the possibilities of the grace-endowed, love-saturated Word.

The Word of God is repeatedly made new for us, and we are made new by the Word. Often the easiest access to the limitless Word is via its simplicity. Some of the most seemingly straight forward passages in the Bible can spark the most in depth discussions and interpretations. It makes sense that simplicity would be an entrance ticket into divine complexity. Theological works are often unapproachable, unless one is the academically inclined type. The Word emboldens fervent witnesses who can enliven the spiritual dimension of scripture, without getting bogged down by words themselves. After all, this is a relationship each of us is cultivating with God and

God is co-creating with each of us, thus the existence of multiple entry ways into the Word in the relationship seems a logical conclusion. When exploring being in God's presence through the Word, no need to worry about understanding it or searching for explanations. That can come later. First, just read the Gospels. Find something that speaks to you...then let it speak to you more. The Incarnate Living Word lives for us, expansively within reach. It is the source of creation and leads us to our mission and vocation. It sanctifies, rectifies, commands, and consecrates. It breathes the sacraments (our foundation, our spiritual-child-of-God base camp) into our being – "being" as both noun and verb.

All of creation is vibrant with the Word. The Word is living – in nature, human beings, and throughout the cosmos. When we enter into mystical union with God, the Word suddenly becomes a new entity and we are catapulted into the deeper recesses of our relationship with Him. We are awakened to it, transformed by it, and fundamentally changed in our perceptions of it. The more we empty our unsurrendered self, the more we are filled with the Word. God initiates in us through the Word. When reading the Word, we are converted by its integral nourishment. The Word is the embodiment of the multiplicities of God's revelation. The Word delivers to us the design of grace.

The Word is a mystical, illuminative, made-flesh reality. By the eternal Word He created everything. In Him all things hold together. We are living on borrowed time with borrowed words. Think of all the stories born, all the prayers spoken, all the whispered worries. Consider how our current technologies have exponentially added to the infinite collection of words. As the supreme origin of all words ever, God's Word is not based on quantities or even qualities. His Word, the Word, is the keeper of the kingdom, the promise of salvation, the hope of the everlasting us, the eternal God who proclaims "I AM."

The Word Made Personal

God's revelation through the Incarnate Word reveals us to ourselves. As with all aspects of the relationship, I could write forever about the Word, yet barely dust the surface of comprehension. The best I can do is share with you the richness of opportunity that God calls you to through His Word. The Word makes God accessible to us in the relationship through a communication that is possible nowhere else. Those who meditate or spend time in contemplation know that different lines of communication open (within and beyond the self). Contemplation is the oxygen of the mystic breathing in God. Often, those whose lives are immersed in the practice of contemplation are delivered into greater depths of conversion. Those who pray know that communication is a fruitful mechanism in the relationship.

Saint Augustine's seamless fusion of the Word into his written words in *The Confessions* transposes his conversion onto the pages. The film *"Full of Grace"* has a similar seamless interweaving of the Word into the dialogue, enhancing and elevating the cinematic format because the viewer is drawn into it by essentially becoming a character on the receiving end of the Word. Priests do not simply preach the Word; they become the conduit of the Holy Spirit, "unleashing the force of the

Word." The prophets inspired bravery and linked the Old Testament to the New Testament. They narrate God's Word, looking back to origin and coming forth to fulfillment. God delivers to us His grace by way of Sacred Scripture, simultaneously infilling us with His Incarnate Word.

Even if everything you just read about the Word makes absolutely no sense, or you have no experience reading it, my hope is that you will at least detect that the *dynamic* of the Word in the relationship is unparalleled to anything in human relationships. There really is no adequate way to convey how inextricably integral the Word is to understanding and experiencing the relationship. In my ongoing conversion, I notice that God uses His Word to speak to me very specifically. For example, after finding my way back to the Catholic Church, I read voraciously. In the silences between, as I was processing what I read and opening myself to truly *listen* to God, He led me with perfect logic into whatever I was to read next that would thread together my thoughts into a deeper understanding of Him, into a more intimate conversation with Him in the relationship. At first, I attributed this to coincidence. But it became so startlingly specific that I understood that He and I were having an undeniable, ongoing conversation and He was allowing my conversion to flow in such a way that there would be no mistaking Him for anything else than the God He is. And, while writing this book, whenever I doubted myself He immediately provided some reassurance that I was on the right track. Homilies I heard from priests, lectures from theologians, or pertinent discussions on the radio would confirm what I was writing. I also noticed that, at Mass on Sundays, the readings and gospels were also, often verbatim, in alignment with my evolving thoughts

the relationship

and insights in our relationship. Even when I went to confession before Mass, I marveled at how often the readings and gospels directly, specifically addressed whatever it was that I confessed. I was not reading the Scripture in advance; it was reading me.

As I have said, in my years away from the Church, I resided in a more abstract spirituality. The closest I can come to defining it would be the philosophy (not the religion) of Taoism. I felt a connection to the Tao, the flow of love in what many call "the universe." But it was impersonal. Yes, there were many serendipitous experiences and seeming coincidences that enhanced the strength of the connection. But it was not a *personal, mutual* relationship. The emptiness that inevitably resulted from the impersonal nature of a philosophy haunted me, especially in moments of stark isolation. The lack of the personal relationship with God was insurmountable. That longing was in my bones and sinews, and I could not find peace without it. Yet I remained trapped in my longing because I could not create the relationship simply by *believing* in God, or by practicing a religion, or by using faith as my sole entry ticket into the relationship. In retrospect, I now understand that God did not want me to be the one to find Him, because He knew that if it was I who did the finding, I would be bound to a human fabricated *idea* of Him, one in which I would stew in my own doubts. He wanted me to *know*, in no uncertain terms, that this is a *real* relationship. Thus, through His invigorating Word, He initiated an energy in my life that is unlike anything I have ever known. He inflated my heart, gracing me with renewed being.

God's Word is assimilated on a cellular level,

book one

intricately and organically. Thus, I do not want to encourage logic and reasoning by way of simply offering narrow definitions or explanations of it. I wish to encourage the *adventure* of the Word, the exploration into the most intimate aspect of the relationship. In this intimacy, we are simultaneously grounded and in a state of constant suspension. This is perhaps not the most comfortable sensation for those who prefer the security of remaining in the realm of sensible logic and need to feel in control where words are concerned. We do well to remember that the dynamics of the relationship often *feel* at once totally familiar and completely foreign. Indeed, whenever we read Sacred Scripture we can also be praying (not just reading it as though it were a set of stories). Prayer, in conjunction with reading Scripture, widens the open skies wherein our dialogue with our Creator takes flight.

When writing about the relationship, I find myself immersed in being logically illogical. My words are liberated, so that the relationship is not bound and gagged. Is it not a paradox that the Word in the intimacy of the relationship is elevated within the boundaries of religion, yet religion, from the birds eye view of secularism, appears to confine us to structure and rules? I was completely floored at how my relationship with God burst forth once I returned to the Catholic Church. The exponential impact of the Word Made Flesh infusion graced the Word, magnifying and assembling it in right order in Church teachings. It is precisely the Word that delivers to us the intrinsic *freedom* inside the structure of religion, because it is by the Word that the structure of religion is rendered dynamic.

Chapter Thirteen ~ Salvation History †

Imagine the incalculable, that which you cannot imagine. The virtually vast, the all consuming, the seemingly in and out of reach pressing down upon you with a force just barely tolerable. Compressed into a stillness by the love that holds together all things, pinned by a benevolent yet debilitating pressure, you are unable to move. Breathing becomes somehow unnecessary. You hear an internal humming, a holy frequency. And just when you are convinced that you can no longer sustain your being and form inside the all, something even more overwhelmingly enormous simultaneously opens you – to all time *and* to the precise moment, wherein you realize that you are only witnessing the minuscule – one particle of one drop's worth of His truth. You are in the infinite and infinitesimal ocean of God's mercy, wherein you know with certainty that all bodies of water, combined with every tear ever shed and to be shed, would not equal one molecule of one drop's worth of His mercy. Like shimmers of moonlight on the tide receding, dancing while pulled and drawn, you cannot sustain your location. You are fastened and floating inside primordial, kinetic, amniotic love. Tiny, translucent waves of darkness and light, fusing into one entity, transfix and cleanse you.

And then a sudden outburst of laughter rises inside and you are made aware of the indisputable truth that *every* evil thought, word, act and *every* moment of pain and suffering, from *all* human existence would not stand a chance of surviving inside even a speck of God's unquantifiable, unimaginable love. The quintessential joke is on you, and nothing could make you happier.

Lest your every molecule simultaneously implode and explode, you close your eyes, uttering ardent prayers in hope of sustaining your physicality. The benevolent, crushing pressure slowly lifts, then recedes into and becomes origin. You wonder if you imagined it. The answer arrives before you can finish formulating the question. With all and only certainty, you know you literally *could not* have imagined it; humans do not have the capacity to imagine or create such a love as this. But we are graced with the ability to choose it.

Are you playing the long game or the short? The sun sets on your every single day and rounds the clock to rise and cycle you through another. Because we live in time, we easily lock into perceptions that are related to time. We add up celebrated birthdays and divvy up our lives into childhood, adolescence, adulthood, old age. We assess our lives within the context of human time, making time into the prison warden. But this forever circling, chasing ourselves throughout this life, constantly arriving at the false point of reference of self, has an invisible cost: it keeps us trapped *in this life*. We labor so hard to find our place, know our purpose, fulfill our obligations, only to discover a vague but incessant lack within, a sense of being fundamentally lost. Even if we live a life full of faith and doing good works, we still must, at some point, shift – inside and out.

the relationship

This shift relates primarily to where we place our focus. Naturally we each tend to focus on *"my life"* – and by that we mean life on earth. The shift happens when we awaken to the notion that our focus is misplaced, that we should be more concerned with our *everlasting life*, our salvation. Everything we do in this physical body and in human life is preparation. The problem does not lie so much in what we are doing with our time, but rather in what we are missing in our time. Our lives are much more important than we realize, but not in a "carpe diem" way. It is more of an "always prepared" way. Carpe diem living fosters a kind of recklessness and detachment from the deeper importance of our lives, as though we should simply live it up because this life is all we get. Carpe diem living is actually exceedingly limited. It is so glued to time, or rather the passing of time, that it keeps us hyper-focused on the present tense to the point where we get trapped by the "moment" and are fooled into believing that truth *only* resides in the moment, thereby limiting truth by fixing it to time. Truth, life in God, has no such limitations. While it is accurate to say "all we have is this moment," it is also true that any given moment (past, present, and future) is always capable of being pointed in the direction of our salvation. That is not to say that what we do here does not matter. It is how we perceive ourselves in what we do that really has impact. If we perceive our meaning as being tied only to this life, guess where our meaning will be tethered. True freedom comes when we make the shift to offer up to God our every moment, internal and external, trusting in His promise of salvation.

God centers us from within a history constantly in the making, one history sustained by truth. Life on Earth is merely the launching pad. For years I prayed, essentially begging God to show me the way in my life. I was attempting to limit God to time and place, and, by extension, was limiting myself to the same. Yet, the task at hand is not for me to abandon my human life and set all my sights forward. The truth requires more of me; it demands reinterpretation, not annihilation. My awareness that my relationship with the eternal God is ultimately about everlasting life reminds me to *listen* for truth rather than working to construct it. It shows me that the dialogue of prayer is better developed if I stop asking for particular answers. And it teaches me that God's patience with me is endless; His fleeting, eternal truth is not there for me to own (hence fleeting), but is forever there for me to receive.

Christ's life and death are the proof and possibility of our own salvation. Christ pours forth in us a new life, one wherein we reclaim our original holiness and justice and are saved by His loving arms nailed to the cross. When we rise to die, our days are numbered. When we die to rise, we honor Christ's sacrifice for us and accept His redemptive love. It takes great courage to face one's own intrinsic earthly unhappiness, especially in this expanding universe where our lives continue to reach out into multiple directions of becoming. Even the most noble of ventures will drain us if we limit their purpose and bind them to this life. All our efforts end up in vain if we do not bind them to the Cross and offer them to Christ. God gave us a beginning in time and space by sacrificing His Son. There, the cross casts a shadow, reclaiming death, as the sun once more rises in the east. Orientation links to purpose, reoriented by the the intricacy of the brilliant design of our Redeemer's brilliance.

the relationship

When I first heard the term "Salvation History" I thought it would make a great name for a Christian rock band. Salvation History is our access to the history of God's plan for our salvation. It is God's gift of promise to mankind. The seven covenants made between God and mediators, as told in the Old and New Testaments, unravel this history. Salvation history is a past, present and future account; it is not simply a history of looking back, but also a living history of now and forever. "Present history" and "future history" sound like oxymorons; the name "history" is not normally attached to something while it is happening, or to something that has not yet happened. Salvation History is revealed covenant truth, the truth of God's plan, which includes our salvation. You might think that sounds like a naive approach, one that is motivated by the sheer fear of death's permanence. But, again, in the relationship, human opinions and decisions about God's plan have no bearing.

Christ was likely not thinking of His own salvation while dying on the cross. He had no need of being saved. We have need. We cannot save ourselves in this life, nor can we make ourselves rise to Christ simply by dying, or by living for that matter. Only Christ can rise within us, awaken us with grace, love us into assumption. When a child dies, the tragedy is related to how much living he or she will miss, and we mourn the loss we will have to bear. We are that child to Christ. If we attach ourselves only to this earthly and sinful life, we die tragically young in His eyes. And He mourns the loss of us because He wanted us to have everlasting life with Him. It is God's *love* moving in us, made manifest by the sacrifice of His Son, that assures our salvation. The Spirit is the internal expression of God's love, a love that is the connective tissue of our redemption. When we seek to live fruitful lives for God while here on earth, we value, treasure, and make the best of the human life He gave us and He revels in our appreciation of His creation. Humanity has always lived within the tension between living and dying, but the tension of the Second Coming is the tension of conversion. There, we are sinners living for salvation, and our only chance of salvation is the Lamb.

One important distinction, and an easy pitfall, is to selfishly seek salvation to the point that our life on earth becomes about accumulating brownie points. When we do this, we put a spin on sin. We begin to work hard at not sinning, but for ourselves more than out of our love for God. We fear punishment more than we regret offending God. We seek reward for not sinning, rather than offering our efforts at purification to genuinely thank our Creator. It is God's love of all that makes us one, not our limited (often divisive) version of love of self and others. When we love God with our totality, we are able to extend God's love, not our agenda-laden version of love. If loving others is demonstrative of loving God, then the salvation of others is paramount. I do not mean that we should withhold a slice of bread and instead only preach to someone who is hungry. Rather, if our gratitude to God is what shines through in our gift of bread, we are also nourishing the person's spirit with our love of God.

Christ lives in us by way of the Eucharist, the stamp of the Almighty. The living relationship is as pre-destined as it is retroactive. God's promise is hopeful, bountiful salvation. Knowing that death has been destroyed inflates my living. I do not have to spend my hours in fretful anticipation of an end, but can trust instead in the beginning that awaits. I am reminded of the value of

the relationship

reckoning, of revisiting the most important questions I asked myself: "Your relationship with God is everlasting – why would you shrink it by attaching it only to your life on Earth? Why would you deny it by living a life where you place disproportionate emphasis on self? Why would you risk sinning to the point of no return? Why would you embrace evil over good? Why would you deprive yourself of everlasting life for the sake of living it up in this life and denying God? Are you playing the long game or the short game?"

The stakes are high.

Part 3

Pathways to Yes

Chapter Fourteen ~ Fiat †

Surrendering one's will to God in the relationship is the perfect example of how easy it is to intellectually understand an idea, yet how very challenging it can be to bring it to fruition. The false self's default response is to defer to its own will. Our learning curve is steep, thus the need for repetition of this theme. Surrendering to God's will does not happen overnight; it is a moment to moment endeavor.

If we look back in this book thus far, we began with a longing for God, deep within our being. He initiated this longing and calls us to conversion. By His grace, revelation, and the Word, we are shaped and shorn into the creatures He intends us to be. But, at some point, it is our turn to give Him our fiat – our truest "Yes!" – and freely sacrifice our will to His. This is what Christ did on the Cross – He sacrificed His will to the Father, for us. We, in turn, are designed to sacrifice our will – to reassign it to Him. Often, our "Yes!" feels like a struggle because we are so entangled in the throes of our own will. Other times, it feels like a relinquishing, an emptying, a relief even. But, regardless of how it feels to us, surrendering our will to God is the greatest act of free will we can make. For it is within this act that we are reactivated to live in God's will, be led by Him, and are freed to be our truest selves. This is the epitome of paradox in the relationship. It is a bold design, if you

the relationship

think about it. I liken God giving us free will to parents giving a teenager a car: crazy proposition, given the teenager, not yet fully matured, is allowed to choose to be reckless with the gift or use it responsibly. So too can we choose to use our free will to our detriment or as a vehicle to spiritual maturity in the relationship.

Surrendering to God's will is both active and passive. It is active in the sense that I use my own will to make the *choice* to surrender. It is passive in that, once surrendered, both my will and my choice are instantly and voluntarily deflated and are removed from my personal control. This often results in anxiety (due to lack of control) and relief (from the pressure of having to do it all myself). Resistance to turning over my will to God is based on my worries and fears about what my life would become if I did surrender. I often lack confidence that I would be capable of doing whatever God asks of me. The simple truth is that all there is to do is say "Yes!" to my desire for Him, for that desire is already and forever residing in me.

Human desire tends to weaken our resolve to surrender our will. Logically, it would appear that allowing ourselves to be led by God would be the easiest way to live (just kick back and let Him steer our lives). Ironically, it is often the most difficult momentum with which we align ourselves. Hitching a ride with desire, on the other hand, is always easy – at least initially. The greater challenge is to fix our desires on the Lord. When we conform our will to His, we are giving Him the greatest gift of self we can offer. He will take the lead from there – *from within our gift of self*. Thus, when we give Him our self, this self that is so gripped by fears, so isolated by doubts, so misguided by the clutches of the world, He accepts our gift and re-gifts to us a self that is renewed and sustained by His loving, living mercy. When we say "Yes!" to our God, He answers in kind.

In moments of lucidity, I realize that, once my fiat is as complete as it can be at any given time, I move into emptiness, making room for God. I get to be co-created in the now with God, *as* He is creating in the world through me. What I do not know has complete equanimity with what I do know – each can take me to God; each can dispose me to grace. God affords us each this unique camouflage to wear as protection, in that all things can blend into and be shaped to work towards His will. All we have to do is say "Yes!" and, once we do, it becomes amazingly easy and fun to pay attention to our growing, transforming self.

Why, if we love ourselves and God, would we not want to recognize Him for His accomplishment of creating us, loving us, saving us? In praising Him, we become whole. God has no ego to feed. He only seeks our love so that He can return it to us in spades. Our love of God need only be a genuine offering, one that is not based on fear of Him. We are each making our own way in this life, overriding what does not work for us, asserting our will before God's, like runaway trains scrambling beneath the stars. Our will runs rampant and can trick us into thinking we are doing God's will. Thus, we best be objective about our motivations. We do well to continuously consider if we are actually just doing our own will and then dedicating it to God. That is the ego's tomfoolery.

When giving our fiat, it is not that we are conceding to a force that is outside us and reigns over us. It is a revelation cooperation. God created us each accurately special. He assigned us each into the timeless precision of

the relationship

time. He wants us to ask Him to manifest His will in our lives. We can invite Him to manifest His will in our lives and open ourselves to welcome it, but we cannot activate it. We can, however, accept God living in our every cell, thought, expression, and action. We then release and offer it all back to Him; we surrender.

> *"You shall love the Lord your God, with all your soul, with all your mind, and with all your strength...You shall love your neighbor as yourself."*
> ~Mark 12:30-31

How can we possibly follow either of the above commandments if our surrender is conditional or incomplete? If we hold back our love for God, we are essentially holding back our love for our true self. This then triggers us to hold back on loving others. The word love here is not meant to be the mere emotional sentiment. Love of God and others is what is expressed when we allow our true self to live unencumbered by the ego. This is impossible to maintain every waking moment, but simply by paying attention we can catch our ego in the act of diverting us back towards the false self, the self who refuses to say "Yes!" and let God lead. When we love God with our totality we are able to extend to others *God's* love, not our agenda-laden version of love.

> *"Thou hast made us for Thyself, O Lord, and our heart is restless, until it finds its rest in Thee."*
> ~ St. Augustine of Hippo

St. Augustine is probably wishing he had a nickel for

every time someone quoted this line. Perhaps what he was getting at is that, when our hearts rest in God, all opposites are reconciled. And the once restless human heart, the waiting heart, is revitalized as it rests in God's heart, and is readied for vocation, mission, and evangelization. Unless supported by the serenity of God, our hearts can only operate in the realm of self-interest. Once we are held in the rest and calm of God, it becomes natural to think of others and to serve. Our self is no longer threatened. We are no longer in competition for God's attention and love. Our "Yes!" opens us to renewed and refined action, energy, and fervor in faith. The gifts God has been longing to give us throughout our entire existence are made manifest and instruct our being to release them to help others. We connect with self in the way that God always intended us to connect – dependent on Him alone. When our hearts rest in God, the last thing we will receive is actual rest. The resting is just the initiation into the purification of our restlessness. Had God created us to sit around, he would not have given us legs. Once our fiat is firm, once we claim it, it becomes a launching pad for God's revelation of our purpose and path. Our interior person, now voluntarily bound to God, moves God into the exterior world so that others may come to know Him through us.

God's will for my life is not hiding inside me; it comes out of who I am in the "I AM." If I am dependent on God to work for Him, then it is He Who calls me to my mission. My response is simply "Yes!" – even when I have no inkling what that "Yes!" might entail. I am destined to this great love to which He is calling me. In His humiliation on the Cross, my humility is born, and I long with a meek heart to find Him. When humility drains me of self so that I become an offering of nothingness, I am

the relationship

made new, into a servant who wills His will only. And, no matter how my heart wanders, I will always redirect its desires towards authentic surrender to Him.

I am nothing if not dependent entirely on Him. Likewise, I am dependent on my nothingness in order to live entirely in Him. Every time my fiat expands, I am brought to greater weakness. And the cycle continues, so that in my weakness I am able to surrender all the more. As I seek, weaken, and wander, I lose track of my will and of needing control over it. Sometimes this results in genuine nothingness and His will moving in me. Other times, the dark puppeteer interrupts to pull and pluck my strings, and I flail helpless and hopeless. My pride is often so persistent that I convince myself that I possess a strength that is beyond human. But, as long as my heart seeks God, my will finds its way home. Included in the fiat, the "Yes!" we embrace, is also the "No!" we assert against all enemies that attempt to move us away from God, be it the tyranny of the ego, damaging secular influences, temptations, or even demonic interference. And, the more skilled we become at detecting all enemy influences, the more we are reminded to remain on the lookout for the subterfuge to come. I find that surrendering my will to God can sometimes be both unnerving and exciting. On the one hand, I have to be on the lookout for pernicious influences. On the other hand, I am a ship sailing the great oceans and God commands the waves. My survival or engulfment is His to decide.

Doing God's will does not mean we simply continue "doing." In fact, ceasing much of the "doing" in our daily lives can be the first stage of entering into God's will. The doing is ultimately God's doing, and we are acting as agents of His will. So we must be patient, in our listening and in our doing. If I am living from within the confines of my own ego, then anything I do will be steered by my own agenda. If I am living from within God's will, everything I do becomes independent of the forces of my ego. That means having no expectations, no need for preconceived results or impact, not being swayed by criticism or praise, and not relying on any attachments. Living within God's will means abandoning myself to the degree that I will become most myself, because I will live precisely as the person He designed me to be. But this is a life-long endeavor and surely I will often lead myself astray.

Even if I readily chose the mission given, it is not self-generated. I cannot simply use my will to decide what God wills for me and then do it. Rather, all doing becomes being. This is essentially the secret to "Love your neighbor as yourself." In order to love yourself, let the love and will of God move through you and into the world. And it is not really up to you to decide how best to "do" so (that approach only keeps you in ego control mode). Rather, if all of your *doing* is in alignment with *being* in a constant state of surrender, you are not attaching any of it to your identity. Rather, all of it is removed from any ownership on your part. Thus, loving myself means allowing my true self to be, and in so being, God frees me to love my neighbor in the same way – as one of God's creatures. All people are equal as such.

No one person can claim ownership of God. The relationship is not ours to possess. We will often be confused and compare our relationship with God to others' relationships with Him. Being in ego mode fosters this competitive attitude. Thus it becomes nearly impossible for us to truly love our neighbor because we

the relationship

either envy the relationship he/she shares with God, or we discount it and focus only on our own relationship, or lack thereof. In order to love your neighbor as yourself, you might first consider loving your neighbor's *relationship* with God as much as your own. That is the only way you can truly see God in another and recognize Him. Otherwise you risk the potential for judgment, criticism, doubt, and hatred to fester like open wounds in the heart.

Consider the power of the relationship – what else but joy could spring forth from the unity of man and his Creator? What is the interior life of God if not joy? The heart that says "Yes!" is renewed because, in God, there is ample room for an ever-expanding fiat. The Catholic Church looks to the Virgin Mary as the absolute "Yes!" because her total surrender opened her womb to the Holy Spirit infusion of the Incarnate Word. In the relationship, our fiat opens the birthing mechanism to being made new in God. Like Mary, who surely struggled as any mother would, we too will be challenged – often. Rest assured that, by faith, we live by the light of the Cross. We are subsumed into the living relationship where we not only share in the mystery, we become it. We are opened to say "Yes!" to the "I AM," the All that Is, from within the all that we are made to be.

Chapter Fifteen ~ ☙ ✝

Stillness, silence, solitude. One in the same, same in the One. Still, silent, alone we grow into the intimacy of the relationship, imbued in the sameness of ourselves in God. He wants us there. He yearns to quiver our beings alive in stillness. He longs to speak our hearts awake in silence. He loves us into fullness of creation in solitude. Without interior intimacy with God, exterior relationships with others remain staid. So often we default to self-absorbed doing and are dismissive of being. Our culture indoctrinates us to be ever active. All our reflex doing so preoccupies us that we no longer take time for being. Even when in prayer and meditation we focus on methods that require proper postures and instructions. Can we do and be at the same time? Can doing come out of being? Or must being be defined and directed by doing? The problem with relativism is that being becomes so tightly bound to doing that both get lost in translation. In the relationship, being is the source of all doing, because it comes from the source of all being – God. Outside the relationship, doing defines being by way of exclusivity. One is better than another for doing more. One has more value as a human being because of what one is doing, rather than who one is.

But what if being and doing are one truth, in sync with God's will. Stillness, silence and solitude are like the

the relationship

waters of Baptism; we are made new. But these "S" words do not come easily for most of us. We are conditioned to perform and achieve, thus slowing down feels counter-intuitive. In my case, little by little, by pausing and decreasing, the me I used to be fell silent, held still. The relationship growing inside me, began to be reflected outside me and I was able to incrementally release my incessant doing. The more I spent time in God's presence, in the silence and stillness connecting us, the greater my understanding of and adherence to the membrane of my existence. A life that was once lived superficially and frenetically, transformed into a respite in my deepest interior being.

Years before I returned to the Church, God began pulling me towards Him by awakening in me an impetus to go sit in the chapel at the nearby Carmelite Monastery. Catholics will know the practice of Eucharistic Adoration (where one sits before the Blessed Sacrament on display in the monstrance). But I had no idea at the time that I was even in an Adoration chapel. I was just drawn to go there and be in solitude in that still and silent space. Even though, to some degree, I was aware of being benevolently prompted to go to the chapel, I spent my time there in deep longing and excruciating anguish. But some small part of me knew to be obedient and go any time I felt the prompt (which ended up being almost daily).

In years past, I had tried things like meditation, communing with nature on long hikes, and getting lost in creative ventures. But each of these ended up being temporary attempts to feel connected – to God, to myself, to others, to life. But as God gravitated towards me in the relationship, I quickly discovered in periods of solitude, silence, and stillness, that I was able to truly reside in the relationship, mostly by virtue of the fact that I was not so preoccupied by doing anything. In fact, I often would sense God calling, and I would hit the brakes on whatever I was doing, and just lie down and be with Him. The only participation on my part was my *willingness* to spend time with Him. And the way I spent this time was by releasing my mind, not trying to think about or understand anything. Rather, I would just be there and, in the midst of my mind's meanderings, God would begin to move in me, speak in me. I would scribble down notes so that later I could reflect on whatever transpired, but mostly I was quiet and still. Listening for God is rather like being at a crowded party and opting to go out onto the balcony, closing the door behind you to drown out the cacophony.

> *"But when you pray, go into your inner room, close the door, and pray to your Father in secret. And your Father who sees in secret will repay you."* ~Matthew 6:6

We tend to interpret noise as being sourced from the outside. I wonder if it is it not more accurate to think of it as the external manifestation of the noise within us. Perhaps the real cacophony originates in the mind and all the noise is a collective projection of human interior chaos and incessant egocentricity. Ironically, each time we turn down the volume externally, it seems to result in an internal increase in volume (the mind makes a racket when it knows it is exposed). Is it any wonder that both

the relationship

sound torture and extensive periods of silence in solitary confinement are methods of psychological warfare? Forced upon prisoners, noise, silence, and isolation can become weaponized.

Is it possible to quiet the external noise without first addressing one's interior clamor? Religions and spiritual practices throughout the centuries have developed techniques for quieting one's mind. While these can be beneficial in many ways, there is a profound distinction between the discipline of quieting oneself during meditation and the surrender of listening to God. The former is often interpreted as an action by the self, for the well being of the self. The latter is a receptive prayer, a giving over of the self. The voice of God opens one to an intimate communication with Divine silence. We do not create silence, we can only receive it. The more one listens to God, the better one becomes able to listen. And in that listening, God's grace beats loudly in the heart.

Existing in silence is its own prayer. Silence is the substance wherein we encounter the false self and embrace the true self – a being, being in silence. Silence has its own kind of buoyancy, governed by the intangible physics of God's presence. Afloat, we are filled and emptied inside silence. More than the absence of sound, silence is sound sustained and absorbed into ever and always present love. Silence is and becomes transformation. One cannot help but feel the interior shift in the God-initiated, prayerful silence. Stillness too induces transformation. I did not come to this way of being with God by myself. He brought it to me, by deconstructing both my outward life and my inward self. As He peeled away the layers of my doing and weakened me, I learned to be still. He did not want me to *try* to listen for Him, hear Him, seek Him. He did not want me to sit up straight and observe my thoughts during meditation, or anchor myself with a word in centering prayer, or recite rote prayers, or "OM" the day away. He just wanted me to be me, in an almost childlike state of freedom of consciousness, wandering in being. Mind you, this is how He moved in the relationship with me. He may move in very different ways in His relationship with you.

In retrospect, I realize God was creating in me these books and other writings. I have always been a writer, but never had I written in this way. I used to write by super imposing my thoughts and ideas and then forming words around them. But all the words I write and have written for and about Him are sourced in an intimacy that is far beyond visceral or intuitive knowing. This is how He moves in us from within the relationship; He meets us at our truest self and opens us to ourselves in Him, and to Him in ourselves. The athlete might describe it as being in the zone. The physicist might translate it as sudden intellectual insights that merge into discovery. A parent might be most in the relationship by loving a child. But these zones and insights and emotions fluctuate, as we are swept away by the distractions and obligations of daily life. If we give the relationship time and space, it moves into our lives and integrates into our being in such a way that we are aware of God's presence as ongoing, rather than in punctuated moments. St. Paul said: "Pray without ceasing." The only way we can do so is by fully embracing the relationship, so that our very living becomes the constant prayer of our being. And if one's entire life is a prayer, ceasing to pray becomes its own prayer – it becomes one more way of experiencing God's presence moving in our lives through His absence in our prayers.

So there I was, weakened, dismantled, wandering into openness of being, not trying to seek or find Him. I was just living the days, the weeks, the years. More and more, I was able to feel Him moving in me in the relationship. Sometimes I would have a thought or awareness, and, as though in conversation with me, He would thread together my thought with one He would deliver directly. Rather than my habitual way of thinking thoughts by applying logic, reasoning, and creativity, I began to register His thoughts as simply descending upon me. They would just suddenly be there, without any effort or instigation on my part. Since I would often jot down notes, He would take over the progression of the line of thinking and I would essentially play the role of secretary. Other times I would begin a conversation in my imagination, perhaps by asking Him a question. For awhile I would imagine what He would say, as I progressed in my line of thinking and inquiry. But then it was as though He would take over and His side of the conversation would move from existing within the limited mechanism of my imagination into a genuine, open exchange. But, unlike a conversation one has with another human being, these conversations were organic, in that they always embodied truth. In other words, no thought or idea of mine could derail them from God's truth.

The more I allowed myself to make time for solitude, to dwell in silence and stillness, the more His presence permeated all parts of my life. It was as though His presence became more concentrated, motivating me from all directions and impacting every aspect of my life. Everything that I have written up to this point, and all that I will write hereafter, comes from residing within His presence and His presence moving within me. All flatness has become round. All dimensions turn and change in the kaleidoscope of being. And every narrow, limited human moment is now amplified by His grace. I breathe in the relationship within a new dimension of oxygen.

When we go into the desert and, from within the silence collect the Word of God, we replenish our life vocabulary. When we arrive in ourselves as He arrives in us, the only thing left to do is be. This is why silence, stillness, and solitude are so beneficial on our journey into living His will. Since there is no valid vulnerability in the relationship with God, speaking of it and writing about it are not bound by any agenda that is not of His will. Stated another way, no author can convert any reader; only God converts – in His time and in His way. So if you feel yourself being moved towards Him at all while reading, know that only He gives buoyancy to the words herein.

In silence, stillness, and solitude we know for certain that having a relationship with God is not some hokey religious notion. And, although faith and belief in God are worthy entry points, with or without them we remain in the relationship. God is always present, available, waiting quietly, patiently, lovingly for us to welcome Him into our lives. He coaxes us tenderly. The relationship is the real reality of being. It is where human *being* becomes divinized, because of the indwelling of the Holy Spirit. And one of the clearest signs God gives us is that, in our beings and lives, whatever is unified and in right alignment with Him seems exceedingly familiar, as though our souls have always known it.

the relationship

> "[God] gave himself to us through his Spirit. By
> the participation of the Spirit,
> we become communicants
> in the divine nature...
> For this reason, those in whom the Spirit
> dwells are divinized"
> ~Saint Athanasius

Chapter Sixteen ~ Passion †

It is no accident that the internal force that drives us to seek God is the same force that leaves us at greatest risk of being lead astray – namely, our passion. Human passion, in its purest form, is the instinctive, visceral, inevitable desire we have to be unified with God. But because this passion is literally uncontainable, more often than not we opt to live it as passion driving us in negative, destructive ways that seem beyond our control. Deep down it is God's love that we seek, a love that far surpasses human love. We instinctively gravitate towards God's love, yet often without even knowing it is what we are seeking. Our passions are jolted from the realization that the fullness of this love we seek is beyond our reach as long as we exist here on earth.

Our continual seeking of the love of God is hard wired into us, leading us to His Passion on the Cross. Christ's Passion is the time and place where all human sin was (and is) consolidated into one sacrificial offering. Think of Jesus as taking all of God's love and funneling it through one act of sacrifice, so that seeking Him becomes the secret to salvation. Were any of us to stand at the foot of His Cross, we would understand that *each* of us is the object of *all* His love. Think about that – if each of us is the object of all of His love, then all of His love exists in the world through each of us. We are the only ones obstructing and preventing that love from being lived in the world.

The paradox of the dynamic of passion in the relationship is best illustrated in the word "passion" itself (derived from the verb "patior" which means "to suffer"). When Jesus suffered out of love for us, His suffering was an act of purified love – not because His love needed purifying, but purified in the sense that it set the bar for human suffering. Put another way, had He not made this sacrifice, we would never have any hope of a life absent of perverted passions. When we stand at the foot of the Cross, our passion is cleansed because we receive the fullest expression of love possible – His sacrifice for us. We are finally and fully loved the way we desire to be loved – beyond any limits. He loves us more than anyone can ever love us, more than we could ever love Him, others, or ourselves. And because He loves us this much, when unified with Him, our ability to love is purified.

In our secular culture, where relativism runs rampant, we have opted to assert control over the uncontainable force of our passion by redefining it as something over which we have ownership and entitlement. Being in the relationship means facing our weakness and lack of control regarding the suffering in this life. Being in the relationship means pointing all our desires and passions towards God and trusting Him to help us transcend our less than holy tendencies. This is not puritanical fear mongering. Our misguided passions lead to all kinds of problems because they are futile attempts at loving ourselves. Human thoughts, perceptions, emotions, and agendas lock the self into dead center (dead precisely because God is not at the center). The false self must die to the death it is already living. But this is not a simple annihilation or exchange of one entity for another. Rather, it is a deeper quest into the primary relationship and personal encounter with the Creator. Christ on the Cross, purifying human sin thru sacrifice, is where our life truly begins; it is where we breathe and feed off His endless love. Any purified love we bring into the world is an extension of His love, rather than an assertion of our own imperfect attempt to love.

Though we cannot possess God's love, we can live and thrive in its abundance. Our need to possess it comes out of our fixation on scarcity. Why is it that we fall prey to the notion that we never have enough, we never *are* enough? Why do we attach ourselves to desires, clinging to them for dear life, even when we know all along that they will run dry eventually? All our fretting is really anguish, disguised as desire. It is the agony of separation from God. But God will not force His love on us. He will not mandate the relationship. It is ours to choose, and once we choose it, we must unravel and expose all our harmful habits and false modes of thinking, desiring, and being. This takes time, but it also happens instantly. Because God is not bound by time, space, or quantity, and because we are not bound by these *in the relationship*, our life is lived in perpetual abundance, whether we experience it that way or not. Thus, our passion in the relationship is an expression of the abundance of God's love for us and our love for Him. Joy finds its home in His present moment.

True joy is connected to our spiritual life, to God's revelation and grace opening our lives. So, while we might experience some version of pleasure through comforts and anything that makes us feel happy, both pleasure and happiness have limits. Joy, on the other

the relationship

hand, is in alignment with our pursuit of perfection. The only true joy is that truth is joy. God is the source; we cannot fabricate it on our own. But if our spiritual life remains barren or misguided, we can never reach the meaning we seek. At present, many of us exist in an anxiousness wherein we are ill at ease in spirit. Human advancements can never produce the innate joy of the spirit of God operating within the souls and lives of mankind. Unlike our limited passions that drive our limited human lives, we need never limit our passion in the relationship. And when we truly understand this, our lives open us – to ourselves and others. We are no longer trapped in ourselves, confined to yearning, disappointment, and loss. And others cease to be the means by which we get what we want and need. We open to others from within the abundance of God's love, and are thus able to interact with others as being the same – children of God. In the relationship, we "never know a stranger." We relate to others by way of generosity and compassion, bolstered by and dependent upon the immeasurable, passionate love and mercy of God.

Chapter Seventeen ~ Assumed and Genuine †

Living on the edge feels good. The thrill of the ride, the ego boost from assumed courage, and the presumption that one is somehow superior – all of these drive the wild heart to risk. Western culture today is telling this story rapid fire. If you really listen to people when they tell you about what they are doing, thinking about doing, and have done, you hear a faint desperation, an undercurrent of hopeful yearning that they are close to finding "the answer" to happiness. And this yearning often drives those who perceive themselves as being brave into a cycle, an addictive desire for deeper meaning and more accomplishments. Many keep soldiering on, pushing themselves into all kinds of extremes. Factor in the new appendage of the cell phone, and suddenly you have a global arena in which to play out the seeming urgency attached to human life. This assumed courage, coupled with the strong secular message "to live life to the fullest – to get everything out of it that you can," often leads us astray.

And then there is all the stuff. We hoard matter as we spin amongst the stars, as if we are saying "While I am alive, I will accumulate that which I am – matter."

the relationship

Binding ourselves to stuff makes us feel a false sense of security in a life that holds no promises (except death). We accumulate "likes" as a way of deeming our worth to others and feeling right in ourselves. We even stockpile stories, obsessing over viral kittens, while at the same time being desensitized by daily human tragedies. And our obsession with fun-seeking has us accumulating experiences, hobbies, thrills, relationships, as we travel in the physical and cyber worlds, always on the go with trips and trends. All of this we do in the name of "*living* life." While there is certainly much goodness in this way of living (for example, people are using the internet to donate to all kinds of charitable causes), this paradigm for secular living and the many mechanisms necessary to keep the engine running takes time. I used to be so busy in my life that the true essence of living eluded me. I did not create myself, thus despite all my supposed living, much of me was slowly dying. I lacked the ability to exist in creation as the purity of being, and instead kept recycling my misery, each time trying to invent my next new life – you know, the one in which I would have it all figured out and *finally* be happy.

I write these books because the stakes are high. The unsustainable nature of matter is a given. Salvation, everlasting life – that is our destiny; a fuller life on earth is a pithy end goal. God is anything but pithy. *Genuine* courage involves confronting our inherent weakness. We are human and frail. Our destructive tendencies render us willing to choose finality over eternity. Perhaps living in limitation breeds limitation. Man has devised a death of his own making, a death in which he unwittingly sacrifices the life God promises to him. When we pump up ourselves with assumed courage, we are actually lacking the genuine courage needed to see ourselves as

book one

we are: limited creatures. We cannot appropriate life simply by living it vigorously. Our life is not ours to keep or control. When we shun God and instead claim ownership of our lives, we must sustain a kind of bravado so that we do not collapse into the reality of our narrow nature. On the contrary, when we offer our lives to God, for His will and purposes, we are able to surrender ourselves to be as He designed us to be: an expression of His all pervasive creating love.

It is no easy task to relinquish our assumed courage and face our certain weakness. The ego finds it a most distasteful venture and will maneuver to keep us pumped up with a false bravado. The ego will remind us that we are our own master, that we know truth, that we are deserving of this fabricated, supposedly full life. And, if we come to admit that our approach is a farce, the ego will again remind us that our time is best spent on living it up in this life – before our time expires. Thus, even if we make room for God in our quiet thoughts, the ego will be sure to distract us so that we do not make enough time for Him in our lives. Consider, for example, how many people of faith are satisfied that setting aside one hour on a Sunday is sufficient (for God and themselves). By design of the collective ego, our lives remain frenetic so that we do not have time to do anything but perpetuate the ego's incessant need for the spotlight. Add social media to the mix and it almost seems that we are fast becoming the architects of our own religion – the religion of documentation. And the mobile phone has become our new Bible. Sure, sharing ourselves with others by posting the minutia of our days can be fun, but we are not God and documentation is not a religion. It is not a question of eliminating the fun in life. It is a question of priorities – are we putting God before ourselves?

the relationship

It takes *genuine* courage to dismiss the ego and put God first. And, even with the courage to do so, we have many bad habits to shed. This does not happen overnight. And it is a normal response to resist weakness, given the secular world deems it abhorrent and we are well trained to avoid it. Over time, however, we learn to stop resisting our weakness, because we begin to see that it is a conduit through which God's love electrifies our lives. God does not desire that we remain in weakness, on the contrary, He uses our weakness as a force of liberation from the prison of the limited, false self.

We can use genuine courage to continuously set aside our ego and observe *how* we are living. With true objectivity, we quickly detect that much of what we do with our lives is inherently vapid. The ego is not God, thus it is incapable of filling our hearts and minds and lives with the *love* of God. You might wonder how living from within God's love will make your life better, especially since it will entail confronting your sinful nature. Sin does tend to amp up life and make us feel like we are having fun. The pleasures of the flesh entice. They are, however, ephemeral. And as they scatter and we scamper to replace them, we remain unfulfilled. Basic logic tells us that God does not "fill" sin. Thus if sinning keeps our lives empty of God, who then is at the helm of the illusion that the only way to live our lives to the fullest is through sin? Take a wild guess.

Right about now, the bravado of assumed courage might be prompting you to close this book. It is difficult to continue a life of sin when you are reminded to see it for what it truly is. And how exactly do we define sin? Is sin a relative concept? It is much easier to accuse others of being repressed religious zealots who live in fear of

God, flagrantly calling out "sinners" to compensate for their own dread of being punished by God. That way, religious people are wrong, you are right, and you can go on living the way you have been living. That is what I did for decades. By redefining the notion of sin, I was able to perpetuate my erroneous ways and utilize them for my own purposes. It felt courageous at the time, as though I was on the cutting edge, living a fuller life than others would dare to dream. But any facade of assumed courage is bound to crumble, and the walls around me did just that.

Genuine courage is not something we give ourselves. It is a grace, and is thus a gift God initiates. But God will not force this gift upon you against your will. Even if He hunts you down (like He did me), He will always allow you to choose Him. And choosing Him is usually something we do by gradation, in stages, slowly slowly. The ego is well embedded and has likely been fortified by years of getting its way in your life. It will not give up easily. But it does become somewhat entertaining to watch your ego duke it out, while God just loves. The ego can defend only its own ephemeral nature. It is in no way strong enough to overpower God's love. What a stark reality when we finally admit to ourselves that we have been so duped by our own ego. The only relevant, genuine courage is the courage to *choose* to love God. What a blessing to know that He will choose nothing else but to love us.

Chapter Eighteen ~ Fragmentation and Unification †

Human life is a compartmentalized, fragmented existence. We divide ourselves by partiality, sometimes placing emphasis on each aspect of ourselves with an implied exclusivity. Thus, when we consider things like our physicality, emotions, psychological behaviors, sexuality, and spirituality, we frequently fail to connect the dots and form an entirety of self. Using this approach where our spirituality is concerned causes confusion. We might even find ourselves trapped by some psychological mechanism that we assume governs the relationship, wherein we spin ourselves into a web, clinging to our patterned behaviors and responses. For example, if you were to latch onto doubting your ability to succeed in life, that psychological mechanism could easily spill into your spiritual life, making you doubt your own ability to trust God.

God can take anything we bring to Him. We are the ones who deprive ourselves if we insist upon operating within the relationship from any particular aspect of ourselves, while ignoring the rest. Just as God does not parcel out His love for us, in loving Him we are called to open our entire being to Him, and all at once. The mechanics of this are not easy to grasp. In a certain way, we do well to abandon the notion of cause and effect in the relationship. As with the dispensing of grace, God does not wait until we become the person He created us to be as a prerequisite of the relationship. He takes us as we are and always makes available to us our deeper dimensions in the relationship. But we obfuscate the relationship whenever we decide to remain mired in particular aspects of our being and lock ourselves into reductionist interpretations of time and reality. We do this both as a reactive response to spiritual struggles and as a way of seeking solutions to human hardships. For example, imagine you have a pattern of behavior wherein you always seek attention because somehow, through some incident in childhood, you harbor a psychological notion that people do not notice you. Now, if you apply that same psychological behavior as a reaction in your relationship with God, you would likely develop a patterned way of seeking God's love. You would revert to thinking there is something you have to *do*, someone you have to *become* in order to earn and deserve God's love.

Paradoxically, both people who hold fast to religion over all else, and people who hold fast to secularism over all else can end up in a similar dead end. For the person who is too attached to religion, living by the rules alone means eventually being worn down by hypocrisy (because no one can measure up to the rules). The secularist who makes his/her own rules is doomed to fail, due to the instability of the many innate contradictions in being human. As I mentioned previously regarding my return to the Catholic Church – it was not the Church that brought me back to the relationship; it was the relationship that brought me back to the Church. Religion becomes a veneer if it is not born out of the relationship. The rules and regulations, the theology and beliefs –

the relationship

these, in and of themselves, cannot infill us with God's love if they are experienced *outside* the relationship. Likewise, denying organized religion does not remove the many contradictions organic to the self. Life separated from religion develops into the religion of the life of self and is, therefore, limited and fragile. As long as we approach any religion or spirituality solely from within our fragmented human state, we disregard the connective tissue to which God desires to secure us, namely the relationship.

If our relationship to who we "are" is one of receiving from God, then we have no identity separate from our dependence on God. It is not as though God plunked each of us here to exist on our own volition. We are receptacles for an accumulation of gifts bestowed, to include the gift of suffering. And everything we receive and have does not constitute our being, but His. We are truly less alive when holding fast to the fragmented self, because unification with God eludes us and we just keep repeating the same patterns. Human pride keeps us tethered to obstinate individuality, tossed about by the changing winds of cultural trends. The relationship *is* unification with God; we cannot create the unity we seek or define the terms – we can only surrender to them. Thus, the longer we persist in maintaining the relationship on our own terms, the longer we deprive ourselves. We are wise to develop the courage to embrace the habit of letting ourselves be surprised by God, by trusting Him to release our limited self and exist in His dimensionless love. God does not compartmentalize His love for each of us. He loves each of us (and all of us) without measure. He lifts into the majesty the mundane. To each of us He gives a life, teeming inside itself, reverberating His love. He calls us each by name and then scrambles the letters so that we can receive Him in every aspect of our complex, kaleidoscopic self.

Chapter Nineteen ~ Adhere To Cohere †

The relationship is the adhesive that bonds; through it we cohere to God. So many different personalities and minds have roamed this planet throughout the ages. Imagine if God intended no personal relationships with us and instead remained an abstraction to His creatures. By logic, if God did not have a unique personal relationship with each of us, how could any of us consider ourselves to be individuals? If all we are were to be *replaced* by God's love-saturated essence, if there was no singularity in the relationship, then all variation in creation would be rendered meaningless. But God does not want us to adhere to Him in the relationship from inside some generic, robotic existence. God thrives on nuance, because through each of us He expresses Himself uniquely. Like the tree lifting its leaves to be glazed by sunlight from multiple angles, God shimmers and shines as He upholds us to awaken in the relationship. And we the leaves, reshaped by the winds and turned by the seasons, grow and change in endless communication with our unchanging Source. This blend of change and stability, of other and same, sustains the balance in all existence.

The biggest threats to religious freedom in our present world all revolve around idolatry. We idolize the human self and are constantly rerouting morality accordingly. The mind struggles to adhere to truth, as interior vision blurs and refocuses. If each self lives according to its own version of the truth, the word truth itself is redefined. Truth, in its purity, is a singular entity. Instead of the singular truth (lived *and* described differently by Christians, Jews, Buddhists, Muslims, etc.) relativism supports the pervasive "every truth for itself/every man for himself" human-made reality. This means that we are all supposed to "tolerate" the many self-invented truths out there, yet no one is allowed to adhere to truth as singular. The self, by way of its singularity, has appropriated the singularity of truth.

The love of God is the only place wherein we can reconcile our opposites. Good and evil, light and darkness, life and death are purified and made whole. God's mercy is both medicine and cure. Our ailment is at once individual and collective. By clinging to self, we confine ourselves to a limited perception of intimacy. This lack of intimacy then seeps into the collective perception, and the relationship with God is exponentially severed. Human arrogance replaces humility. Ironically, we live in denial of our dauntingly fragile existence. Think of all the potential catastrophes we attempt to dodge and weave on a daily basis (wars, pandemics, genocide, environmental destruction, mass scale terrorism). In my view, the best "proof" that God is real lies in the simple fact that we as humans have not completely annihilated ourselves, multiple times over. *Only* a benevolent God can keep humanity in check; we have proven inept at reconciling ourselves. Yet we somehow keep convincing ourselves that we are the ones in charge.

The good news is that, in the relationship, we never cease reaching and arriving. The Lord blesses us inside

the relationship

our restrictions and limitations, so that we may transform within them by being transformed within Him, in the absence and absorption of all boundaries. There is an important distinction to remember: *desire* to surrender is not true surrender – it is desire. While we wait and coddle our personal, impatient agendas, we long to adhere ourselves to the moment that is Him. We long for radical living, yet cannot, independently, adhere ourselves. We can only open ourselves in surrendered choice.

When each of us adheres to God in the relationship, each of us coheres to every aspect of self *and* to every aspect of others. Consider one of your close human relationships. Over time you probably have developed a keen sense of that person's various moods. You recognize, for example, if that person is annoyed, delighted, or introspective. Sometimes the person you care for will look great physically, other times...not so much. You know the subtle changes in the person's inflections and expressions. But in your relationship, while you may love the totality of the person, more often than not you *relate* to different aspects of the person at different times and for different reasons. If the person is cranky, you might keep your distance. If you are sad, you might seek comfort from the person. And both of you may laugh and be joyous at a special occasion.

God does not put certain aspects of a person at the forefront of the relationship; He is unchanging, thus is not governed by our moods and emotional responses. Rather, God in His glory, relates with every aspect of our being, all at once. This is what makes the relationship so special, so nourishing, and so unique. The ego, in all its vain attempts to appropriate and adhere the glory to itself, could never love in totality – itself or anyone else. Likewise, no human being can relate to us from within an entirely open exchange and unconditional acceptance. No human being can embrace every bit of us, all at once. Humans are prone to judging and demanding and compartmentalizing in relationships. But in *the* relationship we adhere to cohere, and the intimacy our beings require is guaranteed. Once we detach from an egotistical notion of having the ability to understand God, we are liberated to live in God's understanding. This capacity for transcendence is the gift we inherit and we are called to share ourselves from within it.

But we do not share it simply by living a human life here on earth. In the relationship, we break apart and are newly adhered to existence. Gravity shifts and we are re-polarized. We are here, in His here. His real presence in our lives becomes our preparation for everlasting unity. We are never alone. Were we to be in the presence of and receive only a partial Christ, we could never know wholeness, unity. With the whole Christ within, we are never without, never outside His calling us to Him. God upholds the wholeness of every being and allows us to access ourselves and others *from within that wholeness*. Here, human beings are released from limitations into the fullness of emptiness. Here arrogance and pride disappear. Joy is purified. Freedom is perfected. Perfection is freed. And from within this transparency, we look into the mirror image of our foretold tale.

Chapter Twenty ~ The Gift In You †

> *"The hardness of God is kinder*
> *than the softness of men,*
> *and His compulsion is our liberation."*
> *~ C.S. Lewis*

A good place to begin, especially if you seek some kind of proof of the relationship, is by identifying the one thing in life that you are compelled to do. "Compelled" might mean the main obligation or duty you are required to embrace (regardless if you want to or not). Or, it can refer to the one non-negotiable thing that is the strongest impulse or driving force in your life. Another way to frame it is by asking yourself: "What is the one thing I *must* do to live as my true self?"

We normally consider what we must do as being restrictive (especially if we are compelled by another to do it). How then, can God's compulsion be our liberation? We cannot make ourselves be the person God created us to be. We can only be that person in His truth. Hence, the one thing each of us must do is the means by which we authentically reside in God's truth; doing and being become one. When identifying your one thing, do not feel caught up by any category. It might be a talent or hobby, or it could be your role as a teacher or parent. But identifying it is only the first step. Once you identify it, ponder a much deeper question: "Why is it the one thing you absolutely must do?" Regardless if it is your obligation to do it, or your desire to do it, asking why is a viable, authentic line of questioning. God will show you everything you need to see about yourself so that you can grow into the truth in your relationship with Him. He is thrilled when we seek His truth inside ourselves. Keep in mind that, even if you are not *doing* your "one thing" at this time in your life, the compulsion may simply be dormant.

I will share my thought process as an example to flesh out this dynamic. It did not take me long to identify the one thing I must do – write. But the line of questioning became very interesting when I began considering *why* I must write. Yes, I want to contribute to people's lives but the truth is, even if no one ever read a word I wrote, I would still be *compelled* to write. I then wondered if it is because I benefit from the creative process of writing. Again, while that is true, I also derive creative satisfaction when painting, but I am not compelled to paint. Next, I considered what my life would be like if writing was somehow taken away from me. I questioned, for example, how I could ever survive if I were to be imprisoned without paper and a writing instrument. I envisioned myself using a sharp rock to scratch words onto all the walls of my cell. It occurred to me that I would die inside the prison of myself, were I not able to write. I call myself a writer not because of the act of writing itself, or the end result, but because it is what I *must* do to live as my true self. It is where I access the depth of God's truth as it exists in and through me. It is where I find the greatest intimacy in my relationship with God (the irony is not lost on me that my truth in my relationship with God means writing books about the relationship with God).

the relationship

    The gift in you is God's truth, wherein the gift of you comes to fruition. Jesus Christ was compelled by the Father to die for our sins. His life before and after His death are intersected by the Cross. And from the gift of Christ crucified, comes our liberation. In the truth of the relationship, nothing can be a lie – not even sin. This does not mean one will never sin again. But it does mean that our *doing* the one thing we must becomes *being* in God's truth, where sin has already been neutralized. Christ on the Cross is where every facet of sin is laid bare. Thus, when doing the one thing we must, God takes us on an odyssey into the reality of truth, where sin is revealed for what it is, and is then deconstructed so that it can no longer mask His truth. We become better able to reorient ourselves any time we stray from our truth in the relationship. And, over time, our attempts to live outside that truth fall by the wayside. Nothing else feels right or real or important. We become better able to notice and avoid harming ourselves or others, and doing anything that separates us from God. Life and death become safe because our will has been liberated by God's truth in ourselves.

    I was startled to realize that, in terms of identifying the one thing I must do, my compulsion was not simply "to live." So I began to wonder how my need to write could supersede my need to live. If I could not write, I could not be me, because God instilled in me an absolute impulse to write. Writing is the gift of God's truth in me, thus it is where I am able to truly *live* and *give* my life to God (it is up to Him if others will benefit from what I write). While I cannot *possess* His truth, by virtue of expressing it in form I am transformed. Writing these books is the vehicle God is using to create in His relationship with me. It is a living *creating*, because as I live and write, He graces me to access and share His truth living in me.

But my ego has to stay out of it. In other words, if I get hung up in pride, needing to receive praise and recognition from others, or to produce results (like selling books), I am no longer living in the truth of God's gift in me. I am usurping the gift for my own purposes. I am placing others before Him in my need for their approval. The ego cannot hold its own in God's truth. Thus, in the one thing you must do, the ego can only tag along for so long. We cannot claim ownership of truth. We can, however, reside in its echo chamber with others who express it in their unique ways through God's compulsion in their lives. There, truth becomes Pentecostal. All of us are speaking in different languages, yet we are able to fully understand one another, for we are expressing the same truth – God's truth.

Likewise, time has no power in the truth of the relationship. For example, in God's truth, all attempts of my will to circumvent the timeline of finishing any of these books is merely demonstrative of my lack of trust in Him. Because it is God's compulsion in me, my writing is liberated beyond space and time in my relationship with Him. This is *why* it is the one thing I *must* do, because it is where God's truth in our relationship joins my life on earth to the everlasting promise of salvation in Him.

You may not be sure what God's compulsion is in your relationship with Him. Take the time to listen – He will guide you. Even though I have always loved writing, the compulsion to write did not fully manifest during the years that I disconnected myself from the relationship. God's truth living in us transforms all aspects of our living. Any cross we are compelled to carry is also liberated

the relationship

by His truth in the relationship. Hardships diffuse. Tears transform. Christ's sacrifice renders our suffering malleable – particles prone to reconfigure into joy.

*I AM compels the relationship as the liberation
of every I am.*

Epilogue †

Earlier, I made the point that my primary motivation for writing these books was based on my own surprise to discover that this is indeed a *real relationship* and that we cannot compare it to our human relationships, because it far surpasses them in every aspect. Having reflected on the dynamics discussed, you can hopefully see that the relationship with God springs forth and delivers a richness to our lives that is impossible to experience on the human to human level (though it will exponentially enhance our human relationships). Even our closest, deepest, most loving human relationships pale in comparison to God's love, forever living in the living forever relationship.

So where does all of this leave us? For those who "sort of" believe in God, but live primarily secular lives, I hope you might ponder how my general description of the relationship shores up with how you live your life where your relationship with God is concerned – beginning with considering if you believe that you have one or not. For agnostics and those of other spiritual disciplines, even if having a personal relationship with the Creator is not an aspect of your practice, I hope reading this book has inspired you to reflect on the dynamics operating in your spiritual life. For the non-believer, perhaps this has given you a peek at the perks of having a relationship with God, so that you are better able to compare that to what you

the relationship

perceive to be the benefits of a life without God. For lapsed Catholics, as I did, you might hear God making a very personal appeal to you to return to Him and the Church. For practicing Christians and Catholics, my wish is that you will be brought into a deeper intimacy in the relationship, one that is fortified by your faith and fiat.

Abraham did not need Theology. God simply spoke to him. People continue to experience "wilderness encounters" with God. Regardless how much we study God, it may have little or no impact on the relationship. The relationship reaches fruition on earth when one makes a complete sacrifice of one's self to God. Complete means body, soul, mind, spirit, emotions, actions, thoughts and on and on. Every minutia of every part of your humanness. Every particle, atom, molecule, every *everything* of that makes you...you. But how? *How* do we surrender our will? It is not enough to simply say it or pray it so. We require the grace of humility. We begin with the awareness of our limitations. We pay better attention to how much we get in our own way when we live ego-driven lives. And we "let go, let God."

We are not source. The vanishing point is not merely a matter of perspective; it draws the eye into the disappearance of orientation. In the relationship, our perspective is not lodged into the tangible. With faith, we trust that God always accompanies us, even when our weakest self fights to cling to pride. At stake is our access to God's joy, which is ours to discover by way of our nothingness, the terrain of humility wherein we relinquish our will. Our surrender is in no way superimposed. Surrender is not a mechanism or tactic. Nor is it a dose of instant courage. It is the *destination* God has always known you would reach. The when, where, and how of your search *is* the relationship. The relationship *is* your surrender. In it, you are sacrificing your entire self. You give the gift of you. It is not simply a matter of naming the sacrifice or believing it or integrating it. It is a prayer so deep, so empty, so lost that *only* God can hear it. The prayer itself is the sacrifice. Your only intention is surrender, regardless of the consequences. Your whole life makes sense in this sacrificial prayer that reverberates in the darkness: "I am Yours." And God's real, viable, palpable answer to the prayer is: "You are Mine."

> *"And I tell you, ask and you will receive;*
> *seek and you will find;*
> *knock and the door will be opened to you."*
> *~Luke 11:9*

I know that all my knocking and seeking culminates and thrives here, in the relationship. All my past inquiries and spiritual endeavors were not in vain. It is not for me to decide how God puts together the pieces of my life. My most relevant decision was (and is) to choose Him. For the sake of checks and balances, consider the following: If you look at the entire contents of this book and strive to prove yourself as being right and me being wrong, you limit both yourself and me. The reverse is also true, if I am the one trying to prove myself right and you wrong. *All* opposites are reconciled in the relationship. Do I live everything I have written herein? Not even close. I am constantly stumbling upon all the ways I am living as a fraud – talking the talk, but not walking the walk. Potential tends to outshine performance. But when climbing a mountain, if we lose our way we do not need to go back to the bottom and begin again. We just need to

the relationship

get back on the trail to ascending. In other words, that which I myself fail to live need not limit that which I do live. In my one person is everything I am not *and* everything I am. God has already reconciled my opposites – He only created *one* me.

That to which we aspire is already recognized, already available – our awareness of it indicates its existence. All any of us needs to do is *be* our true self in the relationship. Every flower lives to grow in accordance with its unique orientation to sunlight. So too does every child of God lean into the divine light to blossom. The hidden symmetry of God will always remain hidden to humankind, because we cannot sustain the density of human living inside massless, divine light. But light has much to teach us. Like the wind, it cannot be tied to any particular plane rotation or source of direction. We do not live to retrofit divinity. If we are to live in the hidden symmetry of God, we live as light in the light of the risen Christ.

Notes †

All quoted passages from Sacred Scripture:
The Bible, The New American Bible, Revised Edition: Washington, DC: United States Conference of Catholic Bishops, 2002. NABRE United States Conference of Catholic Bishops - http://www.usccb.org/nab/bible

(Disclaimer) *Catechism of the Catholic Church*, 2nd ed. (Strathfield, NSW: St Pauls, 2000).

p.42, chapter 7 *Compendium of the Social Doctrine of the Church*. Ottawa: Canadian Conference of Catholic Bishops, Catholic Church, (2005).

p.46, chap. 8 God "calls us each by name." Isaiah 43:1

p.46, chap. 8 A marvelous book, *The Holy Longing*, by Father Ronald Rolheiser, gives an in depth analysis and understanding of our longing for God and His longing for us.
Rolheiser, Ronald. *The Holy Longing: The Search for a Christian Spirituality* (New York: Doubleday, 1999).

p.54, chap. 9 youtube video "Contemplation to Gain Love," Centro Ignaciano de Reflexion y Ejercicios (CIRE), Herman Directed by Rodriguez Osorio, (Bogota, D.C., Colombia, 2009).

p.62, chap. 10 Guardini, Romano, *The Spirit of the Liturgy* (New York: The Crossroad Publishing Company, 1997), 91.

p.65, chap. 10 "No man is an island" is the title of a poem by John Donne.

p.84, chap. 12 St. Augustine of Hippo, *The Confessions*, David Vincent Meconi, S.J. Editor, (San Francisco: Ignatius Critical

the relationship

Editions, 2012).

p.84, chap. 12 Film: *Full of Grace*, 2015; written and directed by Andrew Hyatt; Rekon Productions; USA.

p.84-85, Chap. 12 "unleashing the force of the Word" Homiletic and Pastoral Review
Preaching the Homily and the New Evangelization, June 13, 2015 by Deacon Peter Lovrick
(reference to address given by H. Em. Card. Stanislaw Dziwisz, Archbishop of Krakow, Intervention at the Sixth General Congregation - Thursday, October 9, 2008)

p.100, chap. 13 St. Augustine of Hippo, *The Confessions*, Ibid.

p.109, chap. 15 St. Paul said: "Pray without ceasing." 1 Thessalonians 5:17

p.112, chap. 15 *Catechism of the Catholic Church*, Ibid, #1988

p.114, chap. 16 Patior is a Latin verb.

p.130, The inspiration for this chapter originated from Ronald Rolheiser's DVD series: "*Mysticism, The Heartbeat of God*" (Ohio: Franciscan Media, 2016).

p.130, chap. 20 Lewis, C S. *Surprised by Joy: The Shape of My Early Life.*, (New York: Harcourt, Brace, 1956).

p.142, Suscipe: prayer by St. Ignatius of Loyola:
https://www.loyolapress.com

Stay Tuned... †

The purpose of Book One is to introduce some of the primary dynamics living in the living relationship. In Book Two, we will delve into the dynamics and mystery of sin and suffering in the relationship, wherein love, pain, joy, and hardship collide and are transformed – and we are made new.

To contact author: therelationshipbooks@gmail.com

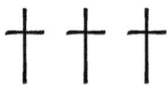

Suscipe

Take, Lord, and receive all my liberty,

my memory, my understanding

and my entire will,

All I have and call my own.

You have given all to me.

To you, Lord, I return it.

Everything is yours; do with it what you will.

Give me only your love and your grace.

That is enough for me.

~ Saint Ignatius of Loyola

www.ingramcontent.com/pod-product-compliance
Lightning Source LLC
Chambersburg PA
CBHW032134040426
42449CB00005B/230